William Hazlitt

Twayne's English Authors Series

Herbert Sussman, Editor

Northeastern University

TEAS 413

WILLIAM HAZLITT
Portrait by William Bewick, 1825
Reproduced by permission of the National Portrait Gallery, London

William Hazlitt

By Robert W. Uphaus

Michigan State University

Twayne Publishers • *Boston*

William Hazlitt

Robert W. Uphaus

Copyright © 1985 by G. K. Hall & Company
All Rights Reserved
Published by Twayne Publishers
A Division of G. K. Hall & Company
70 Lincoln Street
Boston, Massachusetts 02111

Book Production by Lyda E. Kuth
Book Design by Barbara Anderson

Printed on permanent/durable acid-free
paper and bound in the United States of
America.

Library of Congress Cataloging in Publication Data

Uphaus, Robert W.
    William Hazlitt.

    (Twayne's English authors series; TEAS 413)
    Includes bibliographies and index.
    1. Hazlitt, William, 1778-1830—Criticism and interpretation.
I. Title.   II. Series.
PR4773.U64   1985   824'.7   85-8514
ISBN 0-8057-6904-8

For Andrew, Todd, and Kevin

Contents

About the Author

Robert W. Uphaus is professor of English at Michigan State University. He has written numerous essays and reviews, and he has published three books: *American Protest in Perspective* (Harper and Row, 1971), *The Impossible Observer* (University of Kentucky, 1979), and *Beyond Tragedy* (University of Kentucky, 1981).

Preface

William Hazlitt is a writer who has been well served by those who write about him as an individual, but he has frequently been poorly served by those who try to tie him down to a particular literary movement. Cliché that it often is, Hazlitt is truly a transitional figure, if by this term we simply mean that he straddles two periods of literature—namely, the declining traditions of eighteenth-century literature and the emerging traditions of the early nineteenth century, especially what has been called the romantic movement.

Although Hazlitt likes to present himself as a child of the French Revolution, whose political impetus was a stimulus to the literary revolution called romanticism, the truth is he was probably the harshest critic—then as now—of romanticism, largely because it either forgot or denied its revolutionary roots. As we shall see, Hazlitt attacked such key romantic figures as William Wordsworth and Samuel Taylor Coleridge because he felt they became "apostates" to the political cause of reform. In his view, they sacrificed political liberty to the needs of their own poetic programs, conscience to convenience. If Hazlitt had an obsession, it was to find a way to integrate the imagination, as a literary instrument, with the moral and political needs of mankind.

No doubt, to speak of the moral and political needs of mankind may sound lofty and pretentious, but if there was one trait that Hazlitt combated—both in himself and others—it was egotism. All his writings—philosophical, political, aesthetic, literary—are motivated by the desire to expand the reader's sympathetic imagination, to lift us out of an exclusive concern with ourselves into a more inclusive understanding of what it means to be a human being. Not surprisingly, the writer who fully embodies Hazlitt's sense of humanity is William Shakespeare for in Shakespeare's drama Hazlitt finds the fullest expression of the integration of poetic imagination, political liberty, and moral understanding.

Throughout this study I have kept my focus on Hazlitt's comprehensive understanding of the moral, political, and literary uses of the imagination. I do not view Hazlitt's prolific writings as simply occasional, impulsive, and impressionistic. He wrote a great deal, both to support and make a name for himself. He also wrote overmuch, often repeating himself and sometimes being quite unfair. But his energetic output—however repetitious, exasperating, and controversial—reveals a writer with a mission that never changed. From his earliest letters as a schoolboy and young man, we can see that he was preoccupied with the imagination as the key to human understanding. Without the imagination, man was, in his view, no more than the automaton depicted by the modern, material philosophy that Hazlitt attacked throughout his life.

Too often, indeed, Hazlitt's first complete work—*Essay on the Principles of Human Action* (1805)—has not been examined carefully; and yet it is here that Hazlitt presents his first comprehensive version of the sympathetic imagination. From his formulation in this early and complex work, we can see how Hazlitt tests and refines his concept of the imagination in a variety of political, moral, and literary contexts. Reflecting on the course of Hazlitt's career, W. P. Albrecht provides an overview with which I completely agree: "Hazlitt's works fall into four groups, which—in roughly chronological order—are his philosophical writings, his political books and essays, his criticism of art and literature, and the essays of his last decade. . . . Whether dealing with psychological mechanism or with political tyranny, Hazlitt pins his hopes on the power of creative imagination to organize the whole mind and translates its synthesis of thought, feeling, and sensation into laudable moral operations."[1] Hazlitt was a man of many words, but he can easily and accurately be understood in far fewer words. Perhaps indeed, if he had written less, he would be understood better and valued more.

Robert W. Uphaus

Michigan State University

Chronology

1823   *Liber Amoris* and *Characteristics*.

1824   Hazlitt remarries—Mrs. Isabella Bridgwater, a widow. *Sketches of the Principal Picture-Galleries in England*.

1825   *The Spirit of the Age*.

1826   *The Plain Speaker* and *Notes of a Journey through France*.

1828   Volumes one and two of *The Life of Napoleon Buonaparte*.

1830   Volumes three and four of *The Life of Napoleon Buonaparte*, and *Conversations with Northcote*. Hazlitt dies on 18 September at the age of fifty-two in Soho, London.

Chapter One
A Life of Dissent

William Hazlitt was born in Maidstone, Kent, on 10 April 1778. He was the third son of the Reverend William Hazlitt, whose religious practices most closely resemble those of a Unitarian, though nominally he was identified as a Dissenter—that is, as one who did not subscribe to, and frequently opposed, the articles of the Church of England. His father was especially interested in rational religion, so much so that he was unable to accept the doctrine of the Trinity—a position not always welcomed by his congregations. Hazlitt remembered his father as a man who loved "the talk about disputed texts of scripture and the cause of civil and religious liberty."[1] Although the young William Hazlitt would never become a minister, as his father had hoped, he certainly would take on much of his father's temperament and political inclinations, not least of which was his capacity for controversy.

Indeed, because of the Reverend William Hazlitt's singular views, he of necessity became something of an itinerant minister. Because of an early rift in his congregation, the Hazlitts were forced to move to Ireland in March 1780. There Hazlitt's father remained essentially rootless, though typically involved in controversy. Unhappy in Ireland, the Reverend Mr. Hazlitt moved his family to America, where he served as a substitute minister, but was never able for long to maintain his own congregation. Hazlitt's father did help to found the first Unitarian church in Boston, but there is no doubt that he remained a dissatisfied and frustrated man. Once more, in 1787, the Hazlitts moved back to England, where Hazlitt's father took over a Unitarian congregation in Wem, Shropshire.

The young Hazlitt was affected in many ways by the constant moving about and disappointments of his father. At least intellectually, Hazlitt was strongly influenced by his father's independent mind; no less certainly, he was troubled by his father's desire that he turn to the ministry as a vocation. It has been conjectured, though not demonstrated, that the young William may have had a nervous breakdown when he was fifteen. What we do know is that he became, as might be expected from a bright adolescent, a somewhat surly and rebellious young man.

In 1793 Hazlitt was enrolled in the New Unitarian College at Hackney (London). Here he was taught by eminent Dissenters, who provided him with the most advanced and "modern" curriculum available at that time. Though Hazlitt was ostensibly to be trained for the ministry, his interest waned; what he wanted to become most of all was a philosopher. We do know that in 1794 Hazlitt had his first meeting with William Godwin, who was the most influential philosopher of the 1790s because of the significance and notoriety of his *Enquiry Concerning Political Justice* (1793). A year after this meeting—perhaps fortuitously, perhaps not—Hazlitt withdrew from Hackney College, thereby asserting his lifelong intellectual independence at the same time that he rejected his father's wishes.

Even so, through his father's many contacts with such prominent Dissenters as Richard Price and Joseph Priestley, Hazlitt met some of the most famous writers of his time. Two of the most important meetings occurred in 1798. In this year he heard Samuel Taylor Coleridge, soon to become a famous man of letters, preach a sermon on the text "and he went up into the mountain to pray, HIMSELF, ALONE." From this sermon, which is memorably recorded in Hazlitt's essay "My First Acquaintance with Poets" (1823), Hazlitt became enamored of "people of imagination." In the same year he also met William Wordsworth, who was to become the best-known romantic poet. Significantly, and this is a pattern throughout his career. Hazlitt would eventually break with both of these writers, accusing them of becoming "apostates" (that is, traitors) to the cause of the French Revolution. As we shall see, Hazlitt had a habit of alternately being influenced by and then repudiating "father" figures. This is why he had a difficult time keeping friendships, and why he collected more than his fair share of enemies.

Meeting all these famous or soon-to-become-famous people further kindled Hazlitt's ambitions. As yet, his desire to become a philosopher remained just that: a desire. Under his brother's influence (John was a painter), Hazlitt formulated some ideas about painting—a subject he would remain interested in for the rest of his life—and set out to become a portrait painter. In 1802 Hazlitt was commissioned to go to Paris to copy paintings of some of the old masters. He was away for about three months. While he executed his work competently, it became clear that a career as an itinerant painter was neither appealing nor lucrative. A further indication of Hazlitt's basic restlessness and unhappiness is his famous fallout with Wordsworth and Coleridge during this year. Both men accused him of sexual indiscretion, though the details of the allegation to this day remain scanty. Happily, with the loss of these two friends, Hazlitt also began a new friendship with Charles Lamb, noted essayist and humorist, whose affectionate tolerance of Hazlitt's irascibility enabled him to remain a life-long friend.

Beginning in 1805, Hazlitt's career as a writer, if not a philosopher, finally began to take shape. Joseph Johnson, a famous Dissenting publisher, published Hazlitt's *Essay on the Principles of Human Action,* a work on the moral force of the imagination that Hazlitt had been contemplating since his student days at Hackney College. Although the book fell, as it were, stillborn from the press, it was at least a first publication. In the next two years this publication was rapidly followed by the appearance of *Free Thoughts on Public Affairs, An Abridgment of the Light of Nature Pursued, The Eloquence of the British Senate,* and, most importantly, *A Reply to the Essay on Population,* in which Hazlitt systematically examined the moral and political consequences of Thomas Malthus's views on overpopulation. In this latter work, Hazlitt's mature writing voice—the voice of moral outrage and pugnaciousness—started to emerge powerfully

In 1806 Hazlitt also met Sarah Stoddart, a friend of Mary Lamb (sister of Charles Lamb, the famous essayist). They were married on 1 May 1808; of the three children born, only one survived—Hazlitt's second son, William, who was born 26 September 1811. The marriage itself, by all accounts, was at best unsuccessful and at worst a disaster. By temperament and personal habit, Hazlitt was ill prepared for domestic life. The marriage nominally continued until 1822, when he and his wife were officially divorced; but they in fact separated in 1819 and were, for all intents and purposes, estranged long before that.

If Hazlitt was a failure as a husband, he began to be more successful as a writer. By 1811 he was beginning to gain attention as both a lecturer and writer. In that year Hazlitt initially contemplated a series of lectures on philosophy, his principal intention being to discredit what he called the modern, material philosophy. His first lecture was delivered on 14 January 1812, and the series concluded on 28 April. These lectures accomplished at least three goals: they sharpened Hazlitt intellectually, they brought his views to the public's attention, and they prepared him for a career as a controversial writer. By 1812 Hazlitt started to write for the *Morning Chronicle;* this opportunity provided him for the first time with a regular, though hardly lavish, income, and it also brought him into contact with some of the most important writers in London. Moreover, despite the required brevity of journalistic writing, Hazlitt developed ways of enlarging his range of interests by writing short essays, so-called "commonplaces," and dramatic criticism. Through his budding journalistic career Hazlitt shaped his identity as a man of letters whose opinions, however contentious, were clearly to be reckoned with.

In 1814 Hazlitt was released by the *Morning Chronicle,* and began writing for Leigh Hunt's *Examiner* and John Scott's *Champion.* During this year Hazlitt published some of his most important essays: "The Character of Wordsworth's New Poem The Excursion," and several articles on Sir Joshua Reynolds's theory of painting. At this time Hazlitt initiated his special interest in writing personal essays, as well as essays that amount to miniature studies of human behavior. With Leigh Hunt's encouragement, he started a series of "round-table" essays, in which he freely pursued a variety of interests and sharpened his own analytic style. Hazlitt was also quite pleased during this time to be writing for the *Edinburgh Review,* an influential journal for which he had the highest regard.

Well established now as a man of letters as well as a political controversialist, Hazlitt became, from 1816 on, a prolific publisher. Almost all his essays and lectures were collected and turned into books. In 1816 he published *Memoirs of the late Thomas Holcroft,* Holcroft being an important radical figure from the 1790s. In 1817 he published *The Round Table,* collected from his *Examiner* essays, and *The Characters of Shakespear's Plays*—the figure of Shakespeare being, as we shall see, central to Hazlitt's idea of the dramatic imagination. In 1818 he published *A View of the English Stage,* together with his *Lectures on the English Poets,* a work that profoundly influenced the major romantic poet John Keats.

In the meantime, however, Hazlitt continued his attacks on the so–called apostates of the French Revolution. He severely—sometimes excessively—criticized William Wordsworth, Samuel Taylor Coleridge, and Robert Southey. In the course of launching such attacks, Hazlitt established his distinctive combination of literary and political observation, a mix that would most forcefully be expressed in his later volume *The Spirit of the Age* (1825).

In 1819, the year Hazlitt was separated from his wife, he published three works: *A Letter to William Gifford, Esq.* (perhaps Hazlitt's most acrimonious political work), *Political Essays,* and *Lectures on the English Comic Poets.* In the former two works, it is clear that Hazlitt was in a particularly agitated state of mind, possibly because of the constant political controversy in which he was embroiled. Indeed, in 1818 Hazlitt himself was subjected to a vitriolic attack by two writers—John Wilson and John Gibson Lockhart—for *Blackwood's Magazine.* In response to this attack, Hazlitt brought charges of libel, and the case was settled out of court for £100. These attacks, combined with his prolonged divorce proceedings, did nothing to settle Hazlitt's natural combativeness.

Nevertheless, in 1819 he began one of his most important literary projects, entitled *Table-Talk,* a series of essays for the *London Magazine.* The two volumes of *Table-Talk* were published in 1821 and 1822. During this time, unfortunately, Hazlitt also became infatuated with a teenage girl named Sally Walker. From what little can be determined, this young girl was simply a flirt, who caught the eye of a lonely and vulnerable man. The emotional ordeal of being in love with a young girl led Hazlitt, for reasons best known to himself, to publish in 1823 a highly personal account of his dealings with Sally Walker entitled *Liber Amoris.* The most that can be said for this volume is that it greatly reduced Hazlitt's stature in the public eye. A year later Hazlitt remarried, but his second wife, Isabella Bridgwater, left him in 1827.

Despite the many—and seemingly endless—personal disasters in his life, Hazlitt continued to write. In 1824 he began a new series of essays for the *New Monthly Magazine* that he called "Spirits of the Age." Here Hazlitt crisply assessed the major figures of his time in a distinctive and doubtlessly controversial manner. The entire collection of essays was published as *The Spirit of the Age* in 1825. The next year, 1826, Hazlitt published two other works: *The Plain Speaker* and *Notes of a Journey through France.* Then he settled into what he hoped to be a major, possibly culminating, literary project—a life of Napoleon Bonaparte. Through the figure of Napoleon, Hazlitt hoped to express and summarize his own values, moral as well as political. The project, however, did not accomplish what Hazlitt had hoped; and though he did see the first two volumes published in 1828, he did not live to see the last two volumes released in 1830. When he died (18 September 1830) at the age of fifty-two, Hazlitt was unquestionably a major writer—praised by some, repudiated by others, but clearly unforgettable.

Hazlitt's Identity

Hazlitt tried many roles and occupations during his life. First, he was to be trained in the ministry as a successor to his father; then he hoped to be a philosopher, whose views of the imagination would both answer and displace what he called the modern, material school of philosophy. He also thought of becoming a painter, and he gained some notoriety as a public lecturer, and later as a journalist. In a way, all these attempts at varying occupations prepared him for his most distinctive public task, that of being a man of letters.

But Hazlitt's real identity, as distinguished from his occupation, was shaped by the Dissenting tradition he inherited from his father and his father's family, in whom, as Ralph Wardle has commented, "dissent was imbedded in their very bones."[2] Although Hazlitt rejected a career in the ministry, disappointing his father's hopes, there is no question that as a writer he practiced a secular ministry, if you will, based on the humanistic doctrines of his father's Unitarianism. In his angrier moments, Hazlitt condemned the church as an institution, commenting, for example, that "When reason fails, the Christian religion is, as usual, called in aid of persecution" (19:321). But Hazlitt's attack on the church—by which he usually meant the Church of England—should not be misconstrued as a denial of the traditional doctrines of the gospel. Indeed, Hazlitt was simply doing what Russell Richey has described as a distinctive characteristic of the Dissenters: "The Dissenters defined themselves as they were defined in law and in the eyes of English society, in terms of their repudiation of Anglicanism."[3]

The Corporation, Test, and Toleration Acts

To understand the relation between dissent and Hazlitt's biography, we need to distinguish two senses in which Hazlitt was a Dissenter— the legal and the intellectual. By law, as Ursula Henriques has noted, "The political inferiority of Protestant Dissenters was governed by the Corporation Act of 1661 and the Test Act of 1673."[4] Among other things, these acts excluded Dissenters from both the Church of England and from the possibility of holding public office because the Dissenters resisted any alliance between church and state. Moreover, the Church of England excluded Dissenters because their religious beliefs were based, in the words of the Reverend Andrew Kippis (himself a Dissenter), on the "liberty of private judgement and the sufficiency of Scripture."[5]

On the face of it, the assertion of private judgment and the sufficiency of scripture, without any mediation from the church, may not seem to be a radical position; after all such views are at the heart of Protestantism. But what made the Dissenters dangerous—at least in the eyes of civil and ecclesiastical officials—was that they continually challenged the alliance of church and state. In doing so they necessarily attacked the foundation of traditional British institutions. As H. T. Dickinson has clearly demonstrated, the alliance of church and state depended on what Dickinson has called a "Tory theory of order," whose five component elements were "absolute monarchy, divine ordination, indefeasible hereditary succession, non-resistance and passive obedience."[6] We shall see in subsequent chapters that this theory of order is what Hazlitt, throughout his lifetime, condemned as the Tory principle of "Legitimacy."

Against this Tory theory of order, the Dissenters, on the whole, subscribed to a contract theory of the state established by John Locke. Such a contract theory, to quote Dickinson again, "was based on more radical assumptions about the equality of man, the existence of certain universal and inalienable natural rights, and the ultimate sovereignty of the people."[7] This contract theory was the basis, practical and theoretical, of the education Hazlitt received from his Unitarian father, as well as from his teachers at Hackney College.

Now it is true that in 1689 a new law was passed, the so-called Toleration Act, which at least allowed the Dissenters the freedom of public worship in licensed meeting places, though this act continued to exclude the Dissenters from the political rights of those belonging to the Church of England. But the Toleration Act was neither satisfactory to the traditional Tories, who thought it gave the Dissenters too much liberty, nor to the Dissenters, who thought it gave them too little. To quote Hazlitt, any doctrine based on the alliance of church and state, however "tolerant," was wholly unsatisfactory because "Religion cannot take on itself the character of law without ceasing to be religion; nor can law recognize the obligations of religion for its principles, nor become the pretended guardian and protector of the faith, without degenerating into inquisitorial tyranny" (19:323).

There should be no doubt that the Dissenters found the Corporation, Test, and Toleration acts to be no more than the undisguised assertions of tyranny, to which they, as Dissenters, had the natural (as opposed to legal) right of resistance. And resist they did, both politically and intellectually. Indeed, in the late 1780s—during the period approaching the centennial of the Glorious Revolution of 1688—it appeared

that these oppressive laws might be removed; but such a move to reform was completely undermined by the political impact in England
of the French Revolution of 1789, which set off a conservative, not to
say reactionary, response, most memorably voiced by Edmund Burke's
Reflections on the Revolution in France. By the time Hazlitt was in school
at Hackney College, all hopes for removing the Toleration Acts were
smashed. At this time, the London Corresponding Society, an organi-
zation founded by Thomas Hardy in 1792 and pledged to political
reform, was under attack by the British government. In 1793 England
went to war with France, and in 1794 a number of prominent Dissenters and reformists—among them, Thomas Hardy, John Thelwall,
Thomas Holcroft, and John Horne Tooke—were tried on charges of
treason. Although the charges were dismissed, the movement for political reform—greatly stimulated by the French Revolution—was effectively silenced. It is no wonder, then, that "in the later eighteenth
century . . . the rational Dissenters laid greater stress on the right to
intellectual liberty."[8]

Intellectual Dissent

If the laws of England provided little comfort to the Dissenters, they
still had other, more durable resources. It is generally agreed, for example, that the Dissenters were among the best educated and most
intellectually advanced people in England. What they lacked in law
they possessed in learning. Where they were denied religious and political rights, they compensated by asserting their own intellectual
freedom. As Herschel Baker has commented, the Dissenters came to
represent "not so much a unified minority as a certain state of
mind"[9]—and that state of mind is best described as independence of
thought. From the fact of being legally defined as a religious Dissenter,
Hazlitt developed his own voice as an all–purpose dissenter (with a
small "d"). That is, he early and actively sought controversy, consistently assuming a minority position to challenge the prevailing and,
he thought, ossified views of most social institutions.

This dissenting voice, which never wavered, is forcefully expressed
in the preface to *Political Essays:*

I am no politician, and still less can I be said to be a party-man: but I have a
hatred of tyranny, and a contempt for its tools; and this feeling I have expressed as often and as strongly as I could. I cannot sit quietly down under

the claims of barefaced power, and I have tried to expose the little arts of sophistry by which they are defended. I have no mind to have my person made a property of, nor my understanding made a dupe of. I deny that liberty and slavery are convertible terms, that right and wrong, truth and falsehood, plenty and famine, the comforts or wretchedness of a people, are matters of perfect indifference. . . . On these points I am likely to remain incorrigible. (7:7)

Throughout his life Hazlitt remained "incorrigible" about such matters as political liberty, freedom of thought and expression, conscience, and justice. His form of dissent was less religious than political and moral. The major event of his youth, and unquestionably a shaping influence in his life, was the French Revolution, which he describes in his essay "On the Feeling of Immortality in Youth" (1827). Hazlitt writes: "For my part, I set out in life with the French Revolution. . . . Youth was then doubly such. It was the dawn of a new era, a new impulse had been given to men's minds, and the sun of Liberty rose upon the sun of Life in the same day, and both were proud to run their race together" (17:196–97).

Despite the political crackdown on reformists and Dissenters in the 1790s, the influence on the young Hazlitt of the Dissenting tradition, as well as the French Revolution, never diminished. If anything, the reactionary measures of the British government simply strengthened Hazlitt's commitment to political and religious equality. Whether writing as a philosopher, a political journalist, or a literary critic, Hazlitt always espoused liberty and independence of expression. His early published works, however various in subject matter, were built on the the Dissenting intellectual tradition he received from his father and his mentors at Hackney College.

Reflecting on this tradition in his essay "On Court Influence" (1818), Hazlitt reveals a great deal about the formation of his own character. Contrasting the time-serving aura of the royal court with the independence promoted by dissent, Hazlitt observes: "The Dissenter does not change his sentiments with the seasons; he does not suit his conscience to his convenience. . . . He will not give up his principles because they are unfashionable, therefore he is not to be entrusted. He speaks his mind bluntly and honestly, therefore he is a secret disturber of the peace, a dark conspirator against the State" (7:239). Praising the Dissenter's commitment to "independent inquiry and unbiassed conviction" (7:240), Hazlitt goes on to remark that "It is hard for any one to be an honest politician who is not born and bred a Dissenter. Nothing else can sufficiently inure and steel a man against the prevailing prejudices of the world, but that habit of mind which arises from nonconformity to its decisions in matters of religion" (7:239–40).

Hazlitt then concludes the essay with a moving portrait of Dissenting ministers—of men who, like his own father, would "never make an accomplished Courtier" because "They were true Priests. They set up an image in their own minds, it was truth: they worshipped an idol there, it was justice. They looked on man as their brother, and only bowed the knee to the Highest. Separate from the world, they walked humbly with their God, and lived in thought with those who had borne testimony of a good conscience, with the spirits of just men in all ages" (7:241).

Dissenting from Dissent

Clearly, the key words and concepts of Dissenters were principle, conscience, nonconformity, truth, justice, brotherhood. These are the principles and goals that motivated Hazlitt as a man and a writer. Yet, true to his Dissenting background, Hazlitt saw and struggled with the fact that Dissenters could also be smug, self-righteous, and exclusive. Although Dissenters were themselves excluded by law from religious and political privileges, few Dissenters, for instance, argued for the emancipation of Catholics, Jews, and women. Hazlitt was aware of how Dissenters sometimes regarded themselves as an exclusive group; it is against this background that we should understand why, later in his life, he wrote a cautionary letter to his son, William, advising him that

it was my misfortune perhaps to be bred up among Dissenters, who look with too jaundiced an eye at others, and set too high a value on their own peculiar pretensions. From being proscribed themselves, they learn to proscribe others; and come in the end to reduce all integrity of principle and soundness of opinion within the pale of their own communion. Those who were out of it and did not belong to the class of *Rational Dissenters,* I was led erroneously to look upon as hardly diserving the name of rational beings. . . . You will (from the difference of education) be free from this bigotry, and will, I hope, avoid every thing akin to the same exclusive and narrow-minded spirit.[10]

Hazlitt then cautions his son, expressing in a few words his own hard-won knowledge: "Think that the minds of men are various as their faces . . . that there is more than one class of merit—that though others may be wrong in some things, they are not so in all—and that countless races of men have been born, have lived and died without ever hearing of any of these points in which you take a just pride and pleasure" (*Letters,* 219). Raised as a Dissenter, Hazlitt here encourages his son to exercise his right to dissent from his own family and intellectual traditions. His father had asserted his independence as a minister, he asserted his own independence as a writer, and now Hazlitt encourages his own son to practice the freedom and integrity that are the hallmarks of Hazlitt's life and literary works.

Chapter Two
Hazlitt and "Modern" Philosophy

Hazlitt, who initially trained for the ministry, began his authorial career as a philosopher. As much as he might joke about his first philosophical effort, *An Essay on the Principles of Human Action* (1805), calling it a "metaphysical chokepear" (11:102), the truth is this early work formulates a substantial part of Hazlitt's continuing attack on and defense against what he calls the modern, material philosophy. Hazlitt refers to this modern philosophy throughout his career, but he defines it most precisely in several of his early works. For example, in his *Prospectus of a History of English Philosophy* (1809), he identifies "the material, or *modern, philosophy*" (2:113) as principally maintaining that "the mind itself is nothing, and external impressions everything. All thought is to be resolved into *sensation*, all morality into the *love of pleasure*, and all action into *mechanical* impulse" (2:113–14). A further corollary of this modern philosophy, as Hazlitt sees it, is the idea of the perfectibility of man—in Hazlitt's words, "the doctrine of the progressive improvement of the human mind, or of a state of society in which every thing will be subject to the absolute control of reason" (1:201). What the doctrine of perfectibility as well as the modern philosophy depend on is a mechanistic model of mind and society—what is now called behaviorism and social engineering, as it has been popularized by B. F. Skinner in such books as *Walden Two* and *Beyond Freedom and Dignity.* Hazlitt sees that however alluring the utopian goal of the perfectibility model and its celebration of reason, its method is to dismiss such attributes of man as genius, taste, and feeling—those individual characteristics that are the principal nonprogressive, nonmechanistic attributes of man.

In fact, there was much that Hazlitt found attractive in some recent versions of the modern philosophy, but what ultimately disturbed him was its mechanistic view of human nature. Indeed, before we look at Hazlitt's specific analysis of the modern philosophy, it will be useful to examine briefly the most famous and comprehensive expression of this philosophy during Hazlitt's time—William Godwin's *Enquiry Concerning Political Justice* (1793).

Enquiry Concerning Political Justice

Godwin describes the method of *Political Justice* as one that begins "by laying down one or two simple principles, which seem scarcely to be exposed to the hazard of refutation; and then developing them, applying them to a number of points, and following them into a variety of inferences. From this method of investigation, the first thing we are led to hope is, that there will result a system consentaneous to itself; and, secondly, that, if all the parts shall thus be brought into agreement with a few principles, and if those principles be themselves true, the whole will be found conformable to truth."[1] What Godwin hoped to do was to establish a rational basis for the reforms brought about by the French Revolution; but despite Godwin's laudable goal, it soon was clear that many of his contemporaries were not about to entertain a rational discussion of either the French Revolution or reform.

A good example of what Godwin's rational method was up against may be found in a popular work published the same year as *Political Justice*—Hannah More's *Village Politics*. Written in dialogue form, the work aims to discredit just about every modern principle espoused by *Political Justice*. Here, for example, is a typically lopsided exchange between Jack Anvil, a blacksmith, and Tom Hod, a mason:

Tom.   What then dost thou take French liberty to be?

Jack.   To murder more men in one night, than ever their poor king did in his whole life.

Tom.   And what dost thou take a *democrat* to be?

Jack.   One who lives to be governed by a thousand tyrants, and yet can't bear a king.

Tom.   What is *equality?*

Jack.   For every man to pull down every one that is above him: while, instead of raising those below him, to his own level, he only makes use of them as steps to raise himself to a place of those he has tumbled down.

Tom.   What is the *new Rights of man?*

Jack.   Battle, murder, and sudden death.

> *Tom.*   And what is *Benevolence* [a key term in *Political Justice*]?
>
> *Jack.*   Why, in the new fangled language, it means contempt of re-
>   ligion, aversion to justice, overturning of law, doating on all
>   mankind in general, and hating every body in particular.[2]

Clearly, when Godwin used such seemingly neutral terms as "liberty," "democracy," "equality," "the rights of man," and "benevolence"
in *Political Justice,* we should not assume that these terms, in the political context of the 1790s, would easily lend themselves to dispas-
sionate examination. Godwin hoped his method would lead to reasoned
inquiry because he consistently distinguished between reform and revolution, arguing that "if conviction of the understanding be the com-
pass which is to direct our proceedings in the general affairs, we shall
have many reforms, but no revolutions."[3] His method is thus designed
as an intellectual appeal to the "universal sense of mankind" based on
the principle, as Hazlitt observes, "that abstract reason and general
utility are the only test and standard of moral rectitude" (6:132).

How committed Godwin is to "abstract reason and general utility"
may be seen in a section of *Political Justice* entitled "The Voluntary
Actions of Men Originate in Their Opinions." Here Godwin outlines
what finally emerges as a rationally mechanistic method of reform.

The corollaries respecting political truth, deductible from the simple proposition, which seems clearly established by the reasoning of the present chapter,
that the voluntary actions of men are in all instances conformable to the de-
ductions of their understanding, are of the highest importance. Hence we may
infer what are the hopes and prospects of human improvement. The doctrine
which may be founded upon these principles may perhaps best be expressed
in the five following propositions: Sound reasoning and truth, when adequately communicated, must always be victorious over error; Sound reasoning and
truth are capable of being so communicated; Truth is omnipotent; The vices
and moral weakness of man are not invincible; Man is perfectible, or in other
words susceptible of perpetual improvement. (*PJ,* 139–40)

These five propositions—which Hazlitt, however, reluctantly would
dispute—may be described as follows: 1) Man is basically a rational
being, but he can only exercise his rationality when his actions are
voluntary. 2) Man is capable of communicating rational truth, but only
to the extent that his reasoning is voluntary. This confidence in the
ability to communicate truth is later tied to Godwin's concept of "sin-

cerity."[4] 3) Truth is omnipotent—that is, not only all-powerful, but also "when adequately communicated, in so far as relates to the conviction of the understanding, irresistible" (*PJ,* 143). 4) This proposition ultimately emerges as Godwin's doctrine of benevolence, for Godwin is convinced, in opposition to the moral view that man is inherently and unalterably defective, that "Vice and weakness are founded upon ignorance and error" (*PJ,* p. 144). 5) This frequently misunderstood proposition deals with the perfectibility of man. Godwin argues that the doctrine of perfectibility "not only does not imply the capacity of being brought to perfection, but stands in express opposition to it. If we could arrive at perfection, there would be an end to our improvement" (*PJ,* 145).

If we inspect Godwin's method of reform more closely, we can see that it is keyed to the idea that human nature, by which Godwin most often means the mind of man, is inherently progressive or desirous of continuous improvement; and the basis for improvement rests with reason. What basically impedes the steady improvement of human nature, of which the need for reform is both a logical and psychological corollary, is that "government by its very nature counteracts the improvement of individual intellect" (*PJ,* 69). That is, government is in reality "a question of force, and not of consent" (*PJ,* 139), and it is furthermore "the perpetual enemy of change" (*PJ,* 252–53). On this score, as we shall see later, Hazlitt would entirely agree.

Where Hazlitt, however, completely parts company with Godwin's rational method and expectations is in Godwin's paradoxical assertion that "Reform . . . can scarcely be considered as of the nature of action" (*PJ,* 274). Trusting neither the institutions of government nor the initiatives of individuals, Godwin ultimately relies on the mechanistic assumption that "There is a sort of provision in the nature of the human mind for this species of progress" (*PJ,* 273–74). This mechanical urge, which is a drive expressed through but not initiated by individuals, is what Godwin means by perfectibility, and what Hazlitt finally judges as nonsense.

Although Godwin's method is optimistic, it is the optimism of innocence. Hazlitt quickly notices that Godwin's excessive reliance on the "natural" mechanism of reason leaves no room for the individual and seriously underestimates human complexity. As much as Godwin espouses reason as a natural and benevolent force, *Political Justice,* as Hazlitt sees it, inadvertently demonstrates not the strengths but the defects of the modern philosophy. Arguing that *Political Justice* in fact shows "the weak sides and imperfections of human reason as the sole law of human action" (11:23), Hazlitt goes on to explain that "by abstracting, in a strict metaphysical process, the influence of reason or the understanding in moral questions and relations from that of habit, sense, association, local and personal attachment, natural affection," Godwin unwittingly made it appear "how necessary the latter are to our limited, imperfect and mixed being." The example Godwin set for Hazlitt was illuminating but negative; from Godwin's mechanistic method Hazlitt saw conclusively how limiting it is to treat man as a "purely intellectual being" (6:132). By defining himself against Godwin's *Political Justice* and the larger backdrop of the "modern" philosophy, Hazlitt eventually shaped a more affective, though less rational, view of human nature. Hazlitt saw, as Godwin himself later recognized, that any estimate of human nature must take into account the powerful role and influence of human feelings.

Hazlitt's General Critique of the Modern Philosophy

Hazlitt's general critique of the modern philosophy develops in stages. These stages are: 1) Hazlitt's general distinction between two kinds of philosophy; 2) his specific comparison of his own philosophical principles with those of the modern philosophy; and 3) Hazlitt's precise, possibly idiosyncratic, use of such key terms as mind, thought, understanding, imagination, reason, nature, sensation, feeling, experience, power, self-interest, association, benevolence, necessity, sympathy, and prejudice.

On the face of it, this list may seem a bewildering variety of terms, but there is such an internal consistency to his use of the words that one is tempted to say that Hazlitt early on formulated a kind of system that informs his basic political, philosophical, moral, and literary attitudes. For instance, when he resists the modern philosopher's reduction of thought into sensation (the principle of association), morality into love of pleasure (the principle of self-interest), and action into mechanical impulse (the principle of necessity), he widens his philosophical rebuttal into an analysis of all aspects of his culture, as we shall subsequently see in such works as *The Round Table, Political Essays, Table-Talk, Plain Speaker,* and *The Spirit of the Age.*

To begin our examination of Hazlitt's critique of modern philosophy, let us look in detail at his general distinction between two kinds of philosophy. In his preface to *An Abridgment of the Light of Nature Pursued* (1807), Hazlitt comments:

> I know but of two sorts of philosophy: that of those who believe what they feel, and endeavour to account for it, and those who only believe what they understand, and have already accounted for. The one is the philosophy of consciousness, the other that of experiment; the one may be called the intellectual, the other the material philosophy. The one rests chiefly on the general notions and conscious perceptions of mankind, and endeavours to discover what the mind is, by looking into the mind itself; the other denies the existence of every thing in the mind, of which it cannot find some rubbishly archetype, and visible image in its crucibles and furnaces, or in the distinct forms of verbal analysis. (1:127)

The philosophy that Hazlitt calls "experimental" emphasizes the following attributes: It focuses on the understanding and what is determinate. Accordingly, it treats the mind as a tabula rasa—that is, as a blank sheet that passively receives sense impressions. Since this philosophy only gives credence to material experiences, it relies on externally verifiable standards of proof. Such a philosophy Hazlitt rejects as much too limiting. On the other hand, Hazlitt adopts a philosophy of "consciousness," one that begins with and trusts human feelings, however indeterminate they may be. Hazlitt is, therefore, far more attentive to what occurs in the mind. Indeed, by "intellectual" Hazlitt does not mean rational, but mental and internal. Hazlitt's philosophy of consciousness is introspective in the sense that it emphasizes the internal origins of our general notions and perceptions.

Clearly, Hazlitt states a fundamental distinction between a philosophy that places great emphasis on, and attributes most value to, what goes on in the mind of individuals and mankind—which philosophy Hazlitt adopts—as distinguished from a philosophy that gives greater weight and credence to the external world both as a source of information and confirmation of knowledge. Put another way, the philosophy Hazlitt accepts sees the mind as at once active and original, in the sense that it does not depend on external stimulation for its own activity. On the other hand, the modern philosophy sees the mind as basically passive and dependent on external stimuli. Much of Hazlitt's distinction between these two philosophies turns on the key word *experience,* for the one philosophy—that Hazlitt subscribes to—accepts the validity of internal mental experiences as well as external physical experiences. However, the modern philosophy, in Hazlitt's view, depends exclusively on external, materially verifiable experiences and thus proceeds

> from a wrong interpretation of the word *experience,* confining it to a knowledge of things without us; whereas it in fact includes all knowledge, relating to objects either within or out of the mind, of which we have direct and positive evidence. Physical experience is indeed the foundation and the test of that part of philosophy which relates to physical objects. . . . But to say that physical experiment is either the test, or source, or guide, of that other part of philosophy which relates to our internal perceptions . . . is to confound two things essentially distinct. Our knowledge of mental phaenomena from consciousness, reflection, or observation of their correspondent signs in others is the true basis of metaphysical inquiry, as the knowledge of facts is the only solid basis of natural philosophy. (2:114)

Once again, Hazlitt establishes another contrast—that between experience, which he associates with metaphysical philosophy, and facts, which he identifies with natural philosophy. Typically, Hazlitt does not see these two philosophies as contradictory, though they may be rivals. Rather, he contends that an improper understanding of experience has led modern philosophers to ignore or belittle metaphysical philosophy, an attitude that continues to the present day among logical positivists; and he, as a metaphysical philosopher, accepts the importance along with the inherent limitations of natural philosophy. Facts are not enough, nor are they self-evident in Hazlitt's understanding of life; for the origin of these alleged facts is a person whose beliefs, with all their limitations, influence the nature of the facts themselves. Knowledge, in other words, is not only public (as a material philosophy maintains) but also personal, as Hazlitt continually asserts.

Indeed, one of the principles Hazlitt finds most contemptible about the modern philosophy is that "it is not founded on any of the prevailing opinions or natural feelings of mankind. It rests upon a single principle—its boasted superiority over all prejudice. Unsupported by facts or reason, it is by this circumstance alone enabled to trample upon every dictate of the understanding, or feeling of the heart, as weak and vulgar prejudices" (2:215). By "prejudice," as we shall see later, Hazlitt means the habits, customs, and traditions of mankind—their strengths as well as defects—through which people tacitly organize and guide their lives. No philosophy, just as no person, can be free of prejudice in the sense that Hazlitt uses the term; for no person leads an absolutely rational life. Thus Hazlitt argues that "To take away the force of habit and prejudice entirely, is to strike at the root of our personal existence" (4:84).

As we approach Hazlitt's specific comparison of his principles of philosophy with those of the modern school, we should remain aware of three informing principles (some might call them prejudices) that lay behind his analysis. First, throughout all of his writings he adopts the view that "Men's opinions and reasonings depend more on the character and temper of their minds than we are apt to conceive. Not only their prejudices and passions, and the light in which they have been accustomed to view things, influence them much more than the nature of the things themselves; but a great deal depends on the very cast of their understandings, disposing them to imbibe certain prejudices; and confining them to a certain range of thought" (2:113). Such a method of analysis of the distinctive character and prejudices of the person behind the philosophy can, of course, be similarly applied to Hazlitt with illuminating results. For now, however, it is simply important to note this as one of Hazlitt's consistent analytic habits. Second, Hazlitt always responds strongly, sometimes furiously to any suggestion or statement that the mind operates in a purely mechanical manner. Hazlitt continually maintains that "That which we seek, . . . namely the nature of the mind, and the laws by which we think, feel, and act, we must discover in the mind itself, or not at all. The mind has laws, powers, and principles of its own, and is not the mere puppet of matter" (2:116).

Finally, we shall have to follow the important consequences of Hazlitt's subtle and defensible distinction between "an innate knowledge of principles, and innate principles of knowledge" (2:165). Hazlitt readily concedes that John Locke and his followers persuasively argued that we do not have an innate knowledge of principles; but they have not undermined the idea that we have innate principles of knowledge—by which Hazlitt means that "there are certain general principles or forms of thinking, something like the moulds in which any thing is cast, according to which our ideas follow one another in a certain order, though the knowledge, i.e. perception of what these principles are, and the forming them into distinct propositions is the result of experience" (2:165). This distinction is extremely important to Hazlitt's thought because he always assumes that much of human knowledge is tacit; it is "prejudice" in the sense that it frequently exists below the level of consciousness, escaping the grasp of abstract reason. For Hazlitt, writers who deeply, if not fully, tap this level of human experience tend to be geniuses of "nature" and the unconscious, like Shakespeare, whom Hazlitt so avidly celebrates.

The Two Philosophies Compared

Rather conveniently, we can study the specific comparisons between Hazlitt's philosophical views and those of the modern school if we compare the ten points Hazlitt espouses in the *Prospectus of a History of English Philosophy* with the ten points he renounces in his lecture "On the Writings of Hobbes." Although these two listings do not in every case match on a one–to–one basis, they are certainly close enough to provide an accurate grasp of what Hazlitt specifically refutes. We shall see that Hazlitt's basic points focus on the three general areas of thought, morality, and action.

Human Thought.   Regarding human thought, Hazlitt asserts the following principles: 1) "The mind itself is not material"—that is, "thought and feeling do not originate in . . . matter" (2:116); 2) *The understanding or intellectual power of the mind is entirely distinct from simple perception or sensation.* By the understanding I mean that faculty which perceives the *relation* of things. . . . Ideas are the offspring of the understanding, not of the senses" (2:116–17); 3) "The power of abstraction is a necessary consequence of the limitation of the comprehending power of the mind. . . . The only difference between abstract and particular, is that of being more or less general, of leaving out more or fewer circumstances" (2.117); 4) "Reason is a distinct source of knowledge or inlet of truth, over and above *experience*" (2:117); 5) "The principle of association does not account for all our ideas, feelings, and actions" (2:117).

What, one may well ask, does all this mean? It means, first, that Hazlitt keeps mind and matter wholly separate because matter can be described by mechanical laws, but mind can free itself of natural law—an exercise of freedom most often seen in artistic genius. Moreover, the intellectual power of mind is its ability to perceive relations and to be comprehensive; simple perceptions or sensations receive their meaning from the power of the mind that, in effect, converts them into meaningful experiences. This power of conversion is itself dependent on the mind's power of abstraction, which is one of the mind's innate principles of knowledge. In other words, without the mind's initial power of abstraction, which enables it to fit new data into a comprehensible context, all particular ideas and sensations would be diffuse and incomprehensible. Without the power of abstraction, the mind would respond to simple ideas and sensations like an unprogrammed computer; it would not know how to interpret and organize the data it was fed. Consistent with Hazlitt's views that the mind is distinct from matter, has a power distinct from simple perception and sensation, and that one of these powers is abstraction, Hazlitt necessarily distinguishes between reason and experience. Reason acts on, and is therefore different from, the experience it receives. Hazlitt thus refutes the principle of association because it asserts that the mind always responds to experience in a predictable and uniform manner.

If these are Hazlitt's views of human thought, the following are the "leading principles" (2:144) of the modern school that Hazlitt, of course, opposes: 1) "All our ideas are derived from external objects, by means of the senses alone"; 2) "Nothing exists out of the mind but matter and motion, so it is itself . . . nothing but matter and motion"; 3) "Thoughts are single. . . . There is no comprehensive power or faculty of understanding in the mind"; 4) "We have no general or abstract ideas"; 5) "The only principle of connexion between one thought and another is association, or their previous connexion in sense"; 6) "Reason and understanding depend entirely on the mechanism of language" (2:144). Except for Hazlitt's sixth point, which may seem unclear, the principal differences between Hazlitt's views of human thought and those of the modern philosophers are easily seen.

The modern philosophy argues that our ideas derive solely from our sensation of external objects. Since the mind is basically organized by matter and motion, there is no such thing as an internal comprehensive understanding. There are no abstract ideas; rather, the mind works strictly according to the principle of association. Hazlitt, to the contrary, argues that human understanding is distinct from simple perception and sensation. The mind is not material. It is comprehensive, possesses the power of abstraction, and is not limited to the principle of association. For Hazlitt, reason is distinct from experience.

All of Hazlitt's views of human thought may be gathered under the Kantian principle, which Hazlitt frequently quotes, that "The Mind alone is formative" (2:153). Hazlitt calls this concept "the only lever by which the modern philosophy can be overturned" (20:74). He understands Kant's purpose to be "to explode this mechanical ignorance . . . and to admit our own immediate perceptions to be some evidence of what passes in the human mind. It takes for granted the common notions prevalent among mankind, and then endeavours to explain them; or to show their foundation in nature, and the universal relation of things" (1:129).

If the mind is active, formative, comprehensive, and original—as Hazlitt maintains—the modern view asserts a fundamentally mechanistic understanding of how the mind functions. The mind is passive, limited, derivative, and invariably predictable. Moreover—and this bears directly on Hazlitt's condemnation of the notion that "reason and understanding depend entirely on the mechanism of language" (2:136–37)—the modern view advocates the idea of nominalism by limiting the operations of a formative mind to the mechanistic understanding of the operations of language. Nominalism not only denies universal ideas, whereas Hazlitt defends the comprehensive power of understanding together with the power of abstraction, but also it advances the idea that reason is confined to a routinized processing of linguistic particulars or individual sensations.[5]

In this respect, the mind becomes a captive of language, a passive processor of simple sensations; but Hazlitt strongly argues that "If our ideas were absolutely simple and individual, we could have no idea of any of those objects which in this erring, half-thinking philosophy are called individual, as a table or a chair, or blade of grass, or a grain of sand. For every one of these includes a certain configuration, hardness, colour, & c. *i.e.* ideas of different things, and received by different senses, which must be put together by the understanding before they can be referred to any particular thing, or form one idea" (2:280). The formative power, or what Hazlitt also calls the "cementing power of the mind" (2:280), both precedes the experience of particular ideas and sensations—that is why he insists that "reason . . . is over and above *experience*"—and provides them with whatever meaning they are given, the meaning arising from the understanding's relation of things. Reason and understanding, therefore, do not depend on, nor are they limited to, the mechanism of language so much as they actively employ that mechanism to reveal or express the creative operations of mind. In Hazlitt's view, it is a mistake to identify the comprehensive power of mind with the more limited operations of language.

Just as Hazlitt opposes the reduction of human thought to certain passive mechanical processes, so he resists the modern reduction of human morality to motives of self-interest. While he grants the undeniable presence of human egotism, he denies its inevitable determination of human morality on several grounds. First, however, we should examine the differences between his views of morality and those of his opponents.

Morality.   Starting with his earliest philosophical work, *An Essay on the Principles of Human Action,* Hazlitt continually and consistently argues that "there is a principle of natural benevolence in the human mind" (2:118), that "the love of pleasure or happiness is not the only principle of action, but that there are others necessarily implied in the nature of man as an active and intelligent being. The love of truth is one of these" (2:118), and "moral obligation . . . has its foundation in the moral or rational nature of man, or in that principle—call it reason, conscience, moral sense— . . . which, without any references to our own interests, passions, and pursuits, approves of certain actions and sentiments as right, and condemns others as wrong" (2:118). The modern view of morality that Hazlitt renounces can be simply stated: "The sense of pleasure and pain is the sole spring of action, and self-interest the source of all our affections" (2:144). In fact, years later in his "Letter to William Gifford, Esq." (1819), Hazlitt describes the object of *An Essay on the Principles of Human Action* as "to leave free play to the social affections, and to the cultivation of the more disinterested and generous principles of our nature, by removing . . . the metaphysical doctrine of the innate and necessary selfishness of the human mind . . . a principal corner-stone of what is called the modern philosophy" (9:51).

Hazlitt counters the reduction of morality to pleasure, pain, and self-interest by formulating and defending the essential roles of imagination and feeling. He argues that it is through these two key human attributes that we lift ourselves, so to speak, above the mechanisms of pleasure, pain, and self-interest. This strategy of employing the imagination as a central part of morality is perhaps the key contribution he makes in *An Essay on the Principles of Human Action.* The connection between the imagination and feeling is the ability of the imagination not only to conjure up distant objects and experiences, but also to sympathize with—that is, have feeling for—persons and actions with which we are not immediately familiar. It should be noted that Hazlitt's moral understanding of the imagination has eighteenth-century precedents in the sermons of Joseph Butler, as well as in Adam Smith's *Theory of Moral Sentiments.* Like Butler and Smith, Hazlitt asserts the power of benevolence to counteract the principle of self-interest. As J. D. O'Hara has said, "The exercise of the sympathetic imagination serves as an antidote to the sickness of self-love, and it expands one's own character."[6] Hazlitt is also careful to avoid posing the imagination as somehow contradictory to reason; instead he explicitly states "that I do not use the words *imagination* as contradistinguished from or opposed to reason, or the faculty by which we reflect upon and compare our ideas, but as opposed to sensation, or memory" (1:19).

Here, then, are some of Hazlitt's basic distinctions and descriptions of the moral function of the imagination:

The objects in which the mind is interested may be either past, present, or future. These last alone can be the objects of rational or voluntary pursuit; for neither the past, nor present, can be altered for the better, or worse by an effort of the will. It is only from the interest excited in him by future objects that man becomes a moral agent. . . . The mind is naturally interested in its own welfare in a peculiar mechanical manner, only as far as relates to it's past, or present impressions. . . . The imagination, by means of which alone I can anticipate future objects, or be interested in them, must carry me out of myself into the feelings of others by one and the same process by which I am thrown forward as it were into my future being, and interested in it. I could not love myself, if I were not capable of loving others. Self-love, used in this sense, is in its fundamental principle the same with disinterested benevolence. (1:1–2)

This passage expresses the heart of Hazlitt's moral view, and it deserves to be considered carefully. Hazlitt proposes three diverse functions for three aspects of the human mind. In his view, the mind is composed of the imagination, reason, and memory. Reason, as we have earlier noted, is comprehensive and relational, and now Hazlitt suggests it deals basically with objects and experiences *present* to consciousness. The memory (sometimes Hazlitt calls it sensation) deals not only with the *past* generally but also with each individual's past; it is, in short, the most private and subjective aspect of the human mind and therefore is dominated by self-interest. The imagination, however, is the only attribute of mind through which we anticipate the *future;* unlike reason and memory, the imagination enables us to transcend the self-preoccupation characteristic of reason and memory (or sensation). It allows us to conceive of and empathize with other selves and their feelings, even though the basis of this imaginative ability is our intense familiarity, through reason and memory, with our feelings and interests. In his most optimistic estimate of the moral imagination, Hazlitt asserts that "The tendency of civilisation and intellectual intercourse has been to extend the circle of sympathy with the circle of knowledge, to burst the barriers of tribe, nation, and colour, and to extort the confession that wherever there was a kindred feeling, there was a claim to pity, to justice, and humanity" (14:121).

For Hazlitt, then, lack of moral action represents a failure of imagination, an egotistic inability to expand our self-interest into common concerns for others. As Hazlitt suggests, "Our sympathy is always directly excited in proportion to our knowledge of the pain, and of the disposition and feelings of the sufferer" (1:23). Hazlitt thus is not denying the role of pleasure, pain, and self-interest as contributing factors to moral action; he is saying that they are neither the sole nor the original cause of moral action. The imagination, he concedes, is "strengthened in its operation by the indirect assistance of our other faculties"—that is, reason and memory—but it is the imagination alone "which must be the immediate spring and guide of action" (1:23).

On the other hand, the modern school is unrelenting in its assertion of the dominance of self-interest. Against Hazlitt's defense of the moral imagination's benevolence and disinterestedness, this school uses self-love to mean "an exclusive principle of deliberate, calculating selfishness, which must render us indifferent to every thing but our own advantage, or . . . the love of physical pleasure and aversion to physical pain, which would produce no interest in any but sensible impressions" (1:83–84). The modern philosophers, as Hazlitt sees them, make the mistake of either arguing or implying that "we are born with a principle of self-love" (1:12), an idea that makes no more sense than to say we are born benevolent. To Hazlitt, both self-love and benevolence are "acquired" (1:12). Thus, when Hazlitt declares "that the human mind is naturally benevolent, this does not refer to an innate abstract idea of good in general, or to an instinctive desire of general indefinite unknown good but to the natural connection between the idea of happiness and the desire of it, independently of any particular attachment to the person who is to feel it" (2:12).

In the above passage, "independently" is a crucial word, for it assumes, as Roy Park has noted, "a theory of imagination as the faculty of self-transcendence."[7] That is, through the imagination we are able to lift ourselves above self-interest and to sympathize with general feelings regardless of personal attachments or practical consequences. The imagination enables us to feel or sympathize with the condition of people whom we do not know or whom we may even dislike. Similarly, the imagination's ability to elicit feelings—what we call "identification"—may be so powerful that it can lead to adverse practical consequences, such as a jury being convinced of a defendant's guilt yet reluctant or unwilling to find that verdict because they sympathize or identify with the defendant's miserable upbringing.

Hazlitt's final, most compelling strategy for countering the moderns' emphasis on self-interest is to take that term and its apparent opposites—"sympathy," "benevolence," "disinterestedness"—and reinterpret them as two halves of the same coin. Self-love and sympathy depend on each other; their relation is reciprocal for they both contribute to the imagination's ability to function morally. Hazlitt writes:

All that is necessary to my present purpose is to have made it appear that the principles of natural self-love and natural benevolence, of refined self-love and refined benevolence are the same; that if we admit the one, we must admit the other . . . they must stand, or fall together. . . . Give what account you will of it, the effect is the same;—our self-love and sympathy depend upon the same causes, and constantly bear a determinate proportion to each other, at least in the same individual. The same knowledge of any pain, which increases our dread of it, makes us more ready to feel for others who are exposed to it. (1:16,24)

Wisely, Hazlitt refuses "to puzzle myself or my readers with the intricacies of a debtor and creditor account between nature and habit" (1:16), because whether we attribute morality to nature or habit, self-love and sympathy will always remain in a reciprocal relation with each other. The modern attempt to give priority and precedence to self-love and self-interest consciously mechanizes an imaginative process that Hazlitt tends to see as organic (it is an innate principle of knowledge) and developmental—Hazlitt believes that we must actively develop the potential of the imagination, and that this development has marked stages.

Action.   However, to assert both the power of the human understanding as well as the exercise of moral imagination presumes that individuals have free will and can use it. This leads us to Hazlitt's third general area of interest—the matter of our ability to act, to exercise free will. Hazlitt's position is that, first, "the mind is not a mechanical, but a rational and voluntary agent. . . . The mind itself is a real agent, or one cause that activates the will. In this consists its long-contested freedom"; and, second, "the idea of power is inseparable from activity. We do not get this idea from the outward changes which take place in matter, but from the exertion of it in ourselves" (2:118–19). Hazlitt's views are directly opposed to the two modern principles that "the mind acts from a mechanical or physical necessity, over which it has no controul, and consequently is not a moral or accountable agent," and that "there is no difference in the material capacities of men, the mind being originally passive to all impressions alike, and becoming whatever it is from circumstances" (2:144–45).

The first point we need to consider is the meanings—Hazlitt's as opposed to some modern philosophers'—of necessity. Simply understood, the concept of necessity initially meant or referred to a relation of cause and effect—an early version, as it were, of the concept that "for every action there is an equal and opposite reaction." In this sense, the concept of necessity neither states nor implies anything about free will or choice. The modern school, however, tended to alter the meaning of this concept to imply at least two things about choice. The first implication is that necessity really means man is incapable of originating actions; he simply carries out actions for which he is, so to say, preprogrammed. Accordingly, man observes rather than initiates actions and thus is not morally accountable for what he does. The second, no less objectionable version of necessity suggests that circumstances external to man dictate his conduct; this early version of the environmentalist argument again deprives man of the ability to initiate actions or to choose among different courses of action. This position is also an adjunct to the famous Lockean argument that the mind is a tabula rasa that receives impressions but cannot form conceptions or actions on its own.

Hazlitt's response to what he regards as a distortion of the concept of necessity is most precisely stated in his unpublished lecture "On Liberty and Necessity." In this lecture he concedes that the "pure basis" of necessity is "incontestable" (2:245) but that he wishes "to clear away the crust of materialism which has grown over it" (2:245). He explains the "true principle of necessity" as meaning "that the mind is invariably governed by certain laws which determine all its operations; or in other words, that the regular succession of cause and effect is not confined to mere matter" (2:245). As Hazlitt understands it, however, necessity, in its original sense, "is perfectly consistent with human liberty; that is, the most strict and inviolable connexion of cause and effect does not prevent the full, free and unrestrained development of certain powers in the agent" (2:246). Notice that Hazlitt says "development." There is nothing automatic about the exercise of free will;

freedom of choice and will is developed, and a consequence of that development is the freedom to act.

As with his argument that self-love and sympathy are reciprocal, so Hazlitt takes the original, as opposed to the modern, view of necessity and construes it as consonant with the idea of liberty. He argues that "If by liberty be meant the uncertainty of the event, then liberty is a non-entity; but if it be supposed to relate to the concurrence of certain powers of an agent in the production of that event, then it is as true and as real a thing as the necessity to which it is thus opposed, and which consists in the exclusion of certain powers possessed by an agent from operating in the producing of any event" (2:258–59). Properly understood, liberty and necessity describe the concurrence of free will and a particular context or set of circumstances. The mind, as Hazlitt argues, "cannot act without an occasion or ground for acting" (2:267). In other words, we do not exercise our will out of indifference; we have reasons, conscious or unconscious, that are the occasion for our actions. In this instance, Hazlitt is careful to distinguish between two ideas of an "agent," and he clearly favors the one that understands liberty, or free choice, within the context of necessity: "If by an agent be meant the beginner of action, or one that produces an effect of itself, there can be no such thing; but if by an agent be meant one that contributes to an effect, there is such a thing as an agent; and the more any thing contributes to an effect and determines it to be this or that, the more it is an agent" (2:266–67).

Hazlitt's second point regarding human action is as much psychological as philosophical. The idea of power[8] refers both to our general ability to act and to the specific character and quality of our actions. When Hazlitt argues that "the idea of power is inseparable from activity," he means that we are conscious of our exertion of power as moral, not mechanical, agents. But he is also out to establish another premise, whose purpose emerges far more clearly in his essay "Mr. Locke a Great Plagiarist" (1816). Hazlitt establishes the same ten points he customarily associates with the modern system, only he describes the tenth point rather differently from how it is defined in the *Prospectus of a History of English Philosophy*. He writes that in the modern system "there is no such thing as genius, or a difference in the natural capacities or dispositions of men, the mind being originally alike passive to all impressions, and becoming whatever it is from circumstances" (20:75–76). Here the emphasis on power falls more obviously on the idea of genius, for it is genius, finally, that most visibly exhibits the exercise of power and most clearly fulfills the human potential to act freely and originally.

To conclude: This section began with a consideration of Hazlitt's succinct description of the three main principles of the modern philosophy: "that the mind itself is nothing, and external impressions everything. All thought is to be resolved into *sensation,* all morality into the love of *pleasure,* and all action into *mechanical* impulse" (2:113–14). We then considered the implications of Hazlitt's rather cryptic summary of the modern philosophy, and we shall soon examine the practical applications of his philosophical position. Before we do so, a brief summary seems in order so that we can keep in mind Hazlitt's key terms and his continuing counterattack to any position—moral, philosophical, political, literary—that smacks of modernism.

The key terms for the modern philosophy that Hazlitt opposes are association and sensation (with regard to thought), self-love and pleasure/pain (with regard to morality), and passivity, mechanism, and necessity (with regard to action). Against these terms, Hazlitt responds that human thought is formative and comprehensive, that morality derives from the sympathetic imagination, disinterestedness, and benevolence, and that human action originates with power and choice because we are capable of voluntary action.

As we shall see, these distinctions do not represent mere abstract philosophical positions; they have practical, political, and literary ramifications. Moreover, as we consider these consequences we will acquire a surer grasp of Hazlitt's idea of human nature and why he puts so much stress on human feeling and what in modern parlance has been called "tacit knowledge." For Hazlitt, we shall see, *"to feel is to think. . . .* Because the human mind is a thinking principle, it is natural for it to think, it cannot feel *without* thinking" (1:69).

Chapter Three

Responses to the "Modern" Style of Intellect: The Examples of Malthus and Burke

We have looked at Hazlitt's basic philosophical premises, but declaring such premises and enacting them are, of course, two different matters. In Hazlitt's case, we shall see that he was continually able to determine and defend the practical consequences of his philosophical commitments. Principally, he defends these commitments by focusing on not just specific issues but particular persons who represent challenges and sometimes dangers to his views of what is right and good for humanity. As John Kinnaird has aptly commented: Hazlitt throughout his work refused "to regard ideas, any ideas, whatever their political color, as having their source or end in themselves, as free from personal bias, will and circumstance."[1]

Two of Hazlitt's main antagonists were Thomas Malthus and Edmund Burke, the former a live opponent, the latter dead but very alive in Hazlitt's imagination. Interestingly, though Hazlitt carried on a prolonged debate with these men in his writings, they, too, greatly distrusted the "progressive" bias of modern philosophy—what Hazlitt calls "the modern style of intellect [that] inclines to abstract reasoning and general propositions, and pays less attention to individual characters, interests, and circumstances" (9:195). Both Burke and Malthus resisted the modern philosophers' excessive reliance on abstract reason; but Hazlitt parts company with them in their resistance to political and social reform, specifically, the fact and aftermath of the French Revolution. Unlike Hazlitt, they frequently portray political and social reform as a threat to social order and as the likely prelude to revolution.

On the surface, Malthus's principal issue, which he transformed into a fearful specter, was the unfettered growth of population. Initially, Malthus's arguments in his *Essay on Population* (1798) were designed to discredit the doctrines of progress and perfectibility advocated by William Godwin in his *Enquiry Concerning Political Justice* (1793). In fact, however, his *Essay* implicitly attacked the poor—the alleged hotbed of revolution—and provided a defense of the status quo. For Burke, the main issue was more complex but no less menacing: The French Revolution, from which Hazlitt says "I set out in life" (17:196), represented the horrific culmination of an abstract commitment to reason and reform. In Burke's eyes, the French Revolution represented an alteration and degradation not only of Western values but also of human nature itself; in Hazlitt's view the chief significance of the French Revolution is that it "was the only match that ever took place between philosophy and experience" (3:156). We shall consider Hazlitt's responses to these two figures separately and then show how these responses reveal Hazlitt's complex ideology: the interweaving of his political, moral, and philosophical views.

Malthus

Hazlitt's *Reply to the Essay on Population* (1807) originally appeared as a series of letters in William Cobbett's *Political Register.* To these letters Hazlitt added some extracts from *The Essay on Population,* together with his own hostile notes and commentary. As Hazlitt sees it, Malthus's arguments regarding population were less important and, for that matter, less original than the consequences—intended or not—of his position. On the face of it, Malthus's general view of population increases seems reasonable enough. His fundamental principle, Hazlitt writes, "is that population has a constant tendency to become excessive, because it has a tendency to increase not only in a progressive, but in a geometrical ratio, whereas the means of subsistence are either positively limited, or at most can only be made to increase in an arithmetical ratio" (1:215). Hazlitt summarizes Malthus's theory as follows:

First, that the principle of population is a necessary, mechanical thing, that it is the 'grinding law of necessity,' unavoidably leading to a certain degree of vice and misery, and in fact accounting for almost all the evils in human life. Secondly, that all the other sources of vice and misery which have been so much and idly insisted on, have no tendency to increase the necessary evils of population, but the contrary, or that the removal of those different sources of evil would instead of lessening the evils of population, which are much the most important, really aggravate them. (1:246–47)

We in the late twentieth century should be well aware of the cruel gap between the haves and the have-nots; while millions of Americans gorge themselves on fast food, still more millions throughout the world die slowly of malnutrition, famine, and poverty. Such a discrepancy points up one of the consequences of Malthus's analysis that Hazlitt disputes. Hazlitt is quite willing to concede the potentially widening gap between the rate of population growth and the more limited availability of food (thanks to the "green" revolution this gap need not be the case in our time). But he also notices that failure to take action on the condition of the poor, not to say a willingness to accept their condition as "natural" and "inevitable," will have the immoral effect of keeping the poor in "their place," of maintaining things as they are.

Predictably, Hazlitt's response is to the point, if not the jugular vein. Malthus, he says, lectures the poor "on economy, on morality, the regulation of their passions . . . and on the ungracious topic, that 'the laws of nature, which are the laws of God, have doomed them and their families to starve. . . . This is illiberal, and it is not philosophical. The Laws of nature or of God, to which the author appeals, are no other than a limited fertility and a limited earth. Within those bounds, the rest is regulated by the laws of man. The division of the produce of the soil, the price of labour, the relief afforded to the poor, are matters of human arrangement" (11:111). Typically, Hazlitt defends free choice. He concedes that all people live under certain constraints of nature—what he calls "limited fertility and a limited earth." Beyond that, or perhaps in response to these limitations, humans make arrangements; in this case, they create societies, and there is no law of nature—though there are many laws of man—that requires the existence and continued suffering and exploitation of the poor. As Hazlitt in another context observes, "The question with me is, whether I and all mankind are born slaves or free. That is the one thing necessary to know and to make good. . . . Secure this point, and all is safe; lose this, and all is lost" (7:9). The Malthusian position, whether by accident or design, treats the poor as slaves both of their passions and of society—all in the name of what Hazlitt calls "the grinding law of necessity" (1:197) that masquerades as "scientific truth."

This law, which Hazlitt condemns as an unjustified attack on the poor, promotes the view that "population is a naturally growing and necessary evil; that it is always encroaching on and straitening the means of existence, and doing more harm than good; that its pernicious effects are at all times and in all places equally necessary and unavoidable; that it is at all times an evil, but that the evil increases in proportion to the increase of population; and that, therefore, there is nothing so necessary as to keep population down at all events" (1:197). The nearly inescapable conclusion of the "grinding law of necessity" is that the poor are evil, for they embody the menace of overpopulation. They are a threat to social stability. This view, as Hazlitt notices, is in direct opposition to the traditional moral position that luxury, not poverty, produces evil (1:265ff.). Also, the poor, who are clearly the people most in need of assistance and improvement, are treated by Malthus as the chief obstacle to progress and improvement. As Hazlitt remarks, it is bad enough that the poor "labour under a natural stigma; they are *naturally* despised" (1:181). But Malthus further implies that without the poor, life, presumably, might be better for the comfortable, the rich, and the reactionary. Such a position encourages the reinforcement of pride, selfishness, and complacency; or as Hazlitt acutely says, "Formerly the feelings of compassion and the dictates of justice were found to operate as correctives on the habitual meanness and selfishness of our nature; at present this order is reversed" (1:182).

Here we arrive at one of Hazlitt's most singular and laudable characteristics—his refusal to separate politics from morality. Unlike many political theorists of his (no less than our) time—Bentham and Malthus come readily to mind—Hazlitt continually attends not just to the substance, but to the tendency or moral consequences of various political views. Indeed, these tendencies reveal the person behind the argument, and, in Malthus's case, Hazlitt is appalled by the person. He therefore attacks both the ideas and the man, for it is his own view that "the object both of the moralist and politician was to diminish as much as possible the quantity of vice and misery existing in the world" (1:198–99). The evident tendency of Malthus's position is in exactly the opposite direction; excessive population, as Hazlitt understands Malthus, "could only be checked by vice and misery; that any increase of virtue or happiness, was the direct way to hasten it on; and that in proportion as we attempted to improve the condition of mankind, and lessened the restraints of vice and misery, we threw down the only barriers that could protect us from this most formidable scourge of the species, population" (1:199). The political theorist, Malthus, slants his arguments against the traditional moral goal of diminishing vice and misery; evidently the primary "cure" for overpopulation is to allow the poor to starve or, failing that, to promote their starvation by permitting vice and misery to go unchecked. This, as Hazlitt sees it, is a horrific instance of malign neglect.

For good reason, as well as sound humanity, Hazlitt chooses to attack Malthus personally as a man whose "humanity is of the *intermittent sort*" (1:323). No responsive human being could treat the poor with such disregard; worse than implying disregard, Malthus's position, in Hazlitt's view, insinuates this dubious "advantage": "it would be the most effective recipe for indifference that has yet been found out. No one need give himself any farther trouble about the progress of vice, or the extension of misery. . . . When we are once convinced that the degree of virtue and happiness can no more be influenced by human wisdom than the ebbing and flowing of the tide, it must be idle to give ourselves any more concern about them" (1:283–84). To be indifferent is to reject moral action. Though Hazlitt is by no means a cheerful or naive optimist—"I am as little sanguine in my expectations of any great improvement to be made in the condition of human life either by the visions of philosophy, or by downright, practical, parliamentary projects" (1:214)—he still rejects indifference on the quite prudent grounds that "It requires some exertion and some freedom of will to keep even where we are. . . . Take away the hope and the tendency to improvement, and there is nothing left to counteract the opposite never-failing tendency of human things 'from bad to worse'" (1:214).

Clearly, to Hazlitt, the duty of both the moralist and the politician is to resist vice and misery even if—in fact, precisely because—they cannot be checked. Such desires as the need for progress and improvement are goals, not ends, and the purpose of these goals is primarily motivational—that is, to keep people from succumbing to indifference. What finally joins politics and morality is the voluntary commitment to the "spirit of virtue" (1:279)—a quite old-fashioned term to be sure, but one that Hazlitt uses unhesitatingly and precisely. The following statement expresses the cornerstone of Hazlitt's moral and political views; from this position, whose basic assumption is that "what is the work of man it seems in the power of man to confirm or alter" (1:279), Hazlitt never wavers:

Our vices grow out of other vices, out of our own passions, prejudices, folly, and weakness: there is nothing in this to make us proud of them, or to reconcile us to them; even though we may despair, we are not confounded. We still have the theory of virtue left: we are not obliged to give up the distinction between good and evil in imagination: there is some little good which we may at least wish to do. Man in this case retains the character of a free agent; he stands chargeable with his own conduct, and a sense of the consequence of his own presumption or blindness may arouse in him feelings that may in some measure counteract their worst effects; he may regret what he cannot help: the life, the pulse, the spring of morality is not dead in him; his moral sense is not quite extinguished. But our author [Malthus] has chosen to stagger the minds of his readers by representing vice and misery as the necessary consequences of an abstract principle, of a fundamental law of our nature, on which nothing can be effected by the human will. (1:279–80)

Here the collision between Hazlitt's commitment to virtue and Malthus's tendency to indifference occurs dramatically. Several basic distinctions emerge from this confrontation, and though Hazlitt deliberately uses them polemically, that perspective does not diminish their importance. Hazlitt's idea of virtue involves the following assumptions: Human beings are at once limited by and capable of evil. These limitations are the source of much human pain, but we should not permit ourselves to become hopeless; as Hazlitt says, "though we may despair, we are not confounded." We should not be confounded precisely because of our ability to formulate the distinction between good and evil and to attempt to guide our actions accordingly. Above all, as Hazlitt says throughout his writings, we must in every case promote and retain "the character of a free agent" and encourage the exercise of that freedom in the direction of virtue. Malthus, to the contrary, encourages resignation and indifference; he confounds and staggers his readers, as Hazlitt says, "by representing vice and misery as the necessary consequences of an abstract principle [the grinding law of necessity]." Malthus denies or removes the concept of man as a free and responsible moral agent; instead he insinuates his own version of "the devil made me do it." Hazlitt sees that Malthus uses the principle of population as "the great devil, the untamed Beelzebub that was only kept chained down by vice and misery, and that if it were once let loose from these restraints, it would go forth, and ravage the earth" (1:204). Rather than educating his readers, Malthus intimidates them; he blunts our humanity by inducing indifference and apathy in response to the conditions of the poor. The tendency of his essay, as Hazlitt sees it, is to bring virtue to a standstill and to encourage a complacent acceptance of vice and misery as the necessary, "natural" fate of the poor.

Burke

About the general effect of Malthus's *Essay on Population* Hazlitt writes: "It is neither generous nor just, to come in aid of the narrow prejudices and hard-heartedness of mankind, with metaphysical distinctions and the cobwebs of philosophy" (1:182). No such accusation could be brought against Burke, for he, like Hazlitt, knew that human beings are "the creatures not of knowledge, but of circumstances" (1:185). Those "circumstances," as we shall see, reflect a highly complex understanding of human nature, one that Hazlitt intimates when he observes that "Men never act against their prejudices but from the spur of their feelings, the necessity of their situations—their theories are adapted to their practical convictions and their varying circumstances" (8:155). Thus, compared to his hostile response to Malthus, Hazlitt's struggle with Burke is much more complicated and interesting because it occurs at a deeper level. In Burke, Hazlitt encounters an adversary who embodies so many attributes that Hazlitt both respects and desires: an original turn of mind, great depth of feeling, a strong moral purpose, intense regard for civilized values, and, above all, a writing style sustained by a powerful imagination. Ultimately, however, Hazlitt's attitude toward Burke remains ambivalent—now complimentary, now derogatory—because in struggling with Burke, Hazlitt was forced to confront and revise some of his most cherished views. Burke elicits from Hazlitt an awareness of the conflict between his own political commitments to reform, on the one hand, and his tremendous regard for the exclusive or elite power of the imagination.

This tension between the elite power of the imagination and Hazlitt's reformist politics is no doubt what Kinnaird has in mind when he comments that "perhaps Hazlitt's most original idea in literary criticism . . . [is] that poetic imagination is essentially inimical to democracy and democracy to it."[2] Kinnaird's position is overstated. Although Hazlitt recognizes such a tension—he sees it prominently displayed in Shakespeare's play *Coriolanus*—he nevertheless refuses to separate the poetic imagination from the larger needs of the community. Witness, for example, the following attack on Wordsworth's poetry: "As far as I understand the Poems themselves or the Preface, his whole system turns upon this, that the thoughts, the feelings, the expressions of the common people in the country places are the most refined of all others . . . yet, with one stroke of his prose-pen, he disfranchises the whole rustic population of Westmoreland and Cumberland from voting at elections, and says there is not a man among them that is not a knave in grain . . . So much for poetical justice and political severity!" (17:25–26).

Like Hazlitt, Burke did not divide morals from politics; to the contrary, his political views are steeped in moral perspective. W. P. Albrecht is certainly right to observe that "Burke and Hazlitt are alike in accepting the imagination as a moral guide and in distrusting any political scheme based on a selfish calculation of consequences."[3] But unlike Hazlitt, who was consistently antiauthoritarian, Burke argued strongly for the absolute necessity of firm authority, the maintenance of long-standing tradition, and the superior wisdom of institutions over individuals. Hazlitt's ambivalent response can be seen in the two remarkably different "characters" of Burke he wrote.

The complimentary character of Burke was published in 1807 and appeared in Hazlitt's volume *The Eloquence of the British Senate*. The hostile character of Burke originally appeared in an article "Coleridge's Literary Life" published in the *Edinburgh Review* (August 1817). It was also published the same year in the 5 October issue of the *Champion.* The first "character" emphasizes Burke's qualities as an author—in particular, his powerful imagination and resourceful style. The second "character" is much shorter and focuses on Burke the man—especially the ominous moral and political consequences of his views. As we shall see, Hazlitt's ambivalence arises from his great admiration of Burke's imagination and his equally great fear of Burke's personal and political influence.

The "Character of Burke" (1807) expresses all the authorial attributes that Hazlitt admires and desires. What Hazlitt says about Burke in this essay he would never say again with such intensity and conviction about anyone else, except when he was speaking of Shakespeare. Both authors, in Hazlitt's estimation, were men of immense genius, a genius that revealed itself through their comprehensive understanding of human nature. Not only did these two men understand nature generally and human nature specifically; but also their writings expressed and evoked in Hazlitt a quality of experience that he found emotionally irresistible. Although Hazlitt would later disclaim his first "Character of Burke" as "written in a fit of extravagant candour, at a time when I thought I could do justice, or more than justice to an enemy, without betraying a cause" (7:301), the truth is that Hazlitt was too attracted to the power of Burke's imagination to regard him exclusively as the enemy of the cause of reform.

One way of observing his lengthy bout with Burke is to examine and apply a distinction Hazlitt establishes in the first "Character of Burke." Of his discussion of Burke, Hazlitt writes: "I speak of him now merely as an author, or as far as I and other readers are concerned with him; at the same time, I should not differ from any one who may be disposed to contend that the consequences of his writings as instruments of political power have been tremendous, fatal, such as no exertion of wit or knowledge or genius can ever counteract or atone for" (7:308–9). There is the author Burke, a man of great genius whom Hazlitt admires, and there are the "consequences of his writings," which, as the "instruments of political power," have been fatal to reform. Out of this tug of war between the power of imagination and the use of imagination as an instrument of political power will emerge, for Hazlitt at least, a clearer understanding of the imagination and its relation to certain basic truths about human nature. One of these central truths, as Albrecht remarks, is that "*any* doctrine, egotistically insisted on, aborts . . . imaginative completeness."[4]

Let us first concentrate on those characteristics and insights of Burke that make him an author whose style Hazlitt celebrates as "the most perfect prose style, the most powerful, the most dazzling, the most daring, that which went the nearest to the verge of poetry" (12:10). Hazlitt is not merely speaking of Burke's rhetorical eloquence, which is considerable, but also of the grandeur of his ideas and insights that, above all, lifts and enriches our moral sense. Hazlitt assumes that the "power which governed Burke's mind was his Imagination" (7:303), and then suggests that "In judging of Burke, therefore, we are to consider first the style of eloquence which he adopted, and secondly the effects which he produced with it" (7:304). Regarding Burke's style, Hazlitt contends that "he united the two extremes of refinement and strength in a higher degree than any other writer whatever" (7:304). This observation alone places Hazlitt in an awkward position because the general view of Burke, perpetuated by men whose political goals Hazlitt customarily would sympathize with, was that Burke was a "man of disordered intellects, because he reasoned in a style to which they had not been used and which confounded their dim perceptions" (7:305). Later, Samuel Coleridge, a man whom Hazlitt eventually rejected as an "apostate" to the cause of reform, echoes Hazlitt's view of Burke's style when he is reported to have said: "Common rhetoricians argued by metaphors; Burke reasoned *in* them" (20:16). This may seem a fairly trivial point, but Hazlitt realizes that the peculiar power of

Burke's imagination, no less than its sometimes startling effects, reveals itself most conspicuously and forcefully in Burke's unique "philosophical eloquence" (7:304), which combines the refinement of poetry and the reasoning of prose.

In Hazlitt's eyes, Burke had to create a unique style to accommodate and express his deep insights into human nature. Whereas Malthus employs a relatively plain style to convey a simple, intimidating proposition, Burke uses a highly complex style not so much to express as to evoke a profound awareness of "the nature of man" (7:306). Of Burke's evocative style, Hazlitt comments that his "execution, like that of all good prose, savours of the texture of what he describes" (12:12). Hazlitt describes Burke's awareness, which contrasts boldly with the simple-mindedness of Malthus, as follows: "He knew that man had affections and passions and powers of imagination, as well as hunger and thirst and the sense of heat and cold. He took his idea of political society from the pattern of private life. . . . He knew that the rules that form the basis of private morality are not founded in reason . . . but in the nature of man, and his capacity of being affected by certain things from habit, from imagination, and sentiment, as well as from reason" (7:306). Then Hazlitt moves to an analysis and justification of Burke's controversial defense of "prejudice," by which Burke asserts the proposition that we are all more strongly affected by habit and feeling than by consciousness and reason:

Burke was so far right in saying that it is no objection to an institution, that it is founded in prejudice, but the contrary, if that prejudice is natural and right; that is, if it arises from those circumstances which are properly subjects of feeling and association, not from any defect or perversion of the understanding in those things which fall strictly under its jurisdiction. On this profound maxim he took his stand. . . . In short, he believed that the interests of men in society should be committed, and their several stations and employments assigned, with a view to their nature, not as physical, but as moral beings, so as to nourish their hopes, to lift their imagination, to enliven their fancy, to rouse their activity, to strengthen their virtue. (7:306–7)

Hazlitt may hedge a bit when he says about Burke, "I do not say that his arguments are conclusive; but they are profound and *true*, as far as they go" (7:307); yet it is quite obvious that he is attracted to and moved by the profundity and truth of Burke's insights. Before going any further, however, we ought to be certain we know what it is Burke is saying, or at least what Hazlitt thinks he is saying.

The distinction established between men "not as physical, but as moral beings" is the key to Hazlitt's understanding of Burke. Malthus, as we have seen, addresses his audience as physical beings; as Hazlitt caustically says, "Mr. Malthus's whole book rests on a malicious supposition, that all mankind . . . are like so many animals in *season*" (1:236). Burke's understanding of human nature is far more complex: Men are motivated neither by appetite nor by reason so much as they are moved by their affections and imagination. This is why Burke's style is purposely evocative, for it is a style adjusted to an awareness of how responsive and susceptible people are to habit, sentiment, and imagination. Such an affective appeal to the audience's veneration of custom, habit, tradition, continuity—what Burke calls "prejudice"— enables Burke to avoid reasoning us into indifference, as Malthus does. Rather, through his appeal to the audience's imagination and moral nature he moves us toward action and the exercise of virtue. If we look at the last sentence of the passage quoted above, we see that Burke "nourish[es]" our hopes, "lift[s] our imagination," "enliven[s]" our fancy, "rouse[s]" activity, and most importantly of all "strengthen[s]" our virtue. To read Burke is to participate in activity on at least two levels: We work as readers as we respond to Burke's powerful style, and we are encouraged to react strongly to Burke's moral vision as he communicates his understanding of human nature. To read Burke is to participate in a dramatic experience.

We referred earlier to Hazlitt's struggle with Burke. This struggle, we may now see, is reflected in Hazlitt's divided response to Burke as an author and as a political, moral thinker. As Hazlitt's career develops, his political commitments seem increasingly to guide his moral views, and his estimate—or rather fear—of Burke's politics leads him to revise his attitude toward Burke. In a sense it is hard to believe that the man who praised Burke's moral profundity in 1807 could ten years later, and for the remainder of his life, stridently insist on "the vices and infirmities of such a mind as Burke's" and treat Burke as "the poison of high example" (7:226). Such fear, if not hysteria, is not easy to explain unless we recall how strongly Hazlitt was committed to political reform—in particular, to the alleviation of vice, misery, and political oppression. What he most fears, for good reason, is the political power and reactionary tendency of Burke's imagination, even as he continues to admire, albeit grudgingly, Burke's genius as an author.

Perhaps one sentence, which appears in both the "Character of Mr. Burke" (1817) and "Coleridge's Literary Life" (1817), sums up Hazlitt's fear of Burke's power. Hazlitt writes: "He was fitted by nature and habit for the studies and labours of the closet; and was generally mischievous when he came out; because the very subtlety of his reasoning, which, left to itself, would have counteracted its own activity, or found its level in the common sense of mankind, became a dangerous engine in the hands of power, which is always eager to make use of the most plausible pretexts to cover the most fatal designs" (7:228). Where Hazlitt in the earlier "character" celebrates the subtlety of Burke's reasoning, now he condemns it; where he earlier sought to explain and understand the moral complexity of Burke's views, now he only attends to the political consequences of Burke's position; and where formerly the imagination was the key to Burke's genius, now that genius is seen as a slave to political power, especially the power of those opposed to reform. Both in "Arguing in a Circle" (1823) and the *Life of Napoleon Buonaparte* (1828) Hazlitt rejects the style he so enthusiastically praised in the first "Character of Burke." Now we are told that Burke "strewed the flowers of his style over the rotten carcass of corruption, and embalmed it in immortal prose: he contrived, by the force of artful invective and misapplied epithets, to persuade the people of England that Liberty was an illiberal, hollow sound; that humanity was a barbarous invention, that prejudices were the test of truth; that reason was a strumpet, and right a fiction" (19:271–72; 13.50–51).

At the deepest level, then, the central issue that Burke raises in Hazlitt's mind is the nature and use of imagination, both as an expression of genius and as a potential instrument of moral and political power. In addressing his audience as "physical" beings, Malthus made a limited appeal to reason, manipulating ratios to give his observations on population the aura, if not the substance, of natural law and scientific objectivity. Accordingly, Malthus's position was more easily countered, simply because it relied on a fear of the future. But Burke's appeal was far more extensive, for he addressed his readers as moral beings whose ties were much stronger to the past and present than to fear of the future. Although Hazlitt eventually repudiated Burke's politics, he could not reject the power of Burke's literary imagination nor could he easily dismiss the profundity of Burke's moral vision. No discussion of Hazlitt's response to Burke would be complete without examining how Burke's general understanding and defense of prejudice—what more accurately should be called "tacit knowledge"—shaped Hazlitt's basic view of human nature and the functions of the imagination.

Tacit Knowledge and Human Nature

In his book *The Tacit Dimension,* Michael Polanyi develops the concept of "tacit knowledge," a concept quite similar to Burke's explanation and Hazlitt's endorsement of the idea of prejudice. Polanyi's concept of "tacit knowledge" is based on the idea that "we know a great deal that we *cannot tell*" and that the way we initially acquire knowledge is through our ability and willingness to participate in "indwelling," which, in Polanyi's words, "requires us to believe before we know, and in order that we may know." This position further asserts that "confidence in authority is indispensable for the transmission of any human culture,"[5] and it repudiates the idea that human motivation and behavior are best explained by the critical use of reason. Interestingly, like Hazlitt, Polanyi sees Burke's writings as an alternative to the ideal of critical objectivity. Polanyi instructively observes: "I believe that the new self-determination of man can be saved from destroying itself only by recognizing its own limits in an authoritative traditional framework which upholds it. Tom Paine would proclaim the right of each generation to determine its institutions anew. . . . [But] the ideas of Tom Paine can be saved from self-destruction only by a conscious reaffirmation of traditional continuity . . . by the kind of traditionalism taught by Paine's opponent, Edmund Burke."[6]

Now Hazlitt, as we have seen, greatly distrusts the modern style of intellect, which relies excessively on abstract reason and general propositions, while he warmly praises Burke's "profound maxim" about prejudice because it accommodates "individual character, interests, and circumstances" (7:306). Just as Polanyi vigorously maintains that "tacit knowledge dwells in our awareness of particulars"—a fact Malthus never understood—so Burke and Hazlitt, as radically different as their political views surely are, build their understanding of human nature from the particular fact of man's affective nature. "Feeling," as Roy Park comments, "is the most important single factor in Hazlitt's distrust of abstraction."[7] How this affective nature relates to tacit knowledge is incisively expressed by Hazlitt in a variety of contexts.

First, we need to establish explicitly Hazlitt's general understanding of reason, a faculty he does not reject so much as think its part in human nature seriously overestimated. In "The New School of Reform" (1826), subtitled "A Dialogue between a Rationalist and a Sentimentalist," Hazlitt sides with the sentimentalist, asserting that reason "may signify any one of three things, all of them insufficient as tests and standards of moral sentiment, or (if that word displeases) of moral conduct:—1. Abstract truth, as distinct from local impressions or individual partialities; 2. Calm, inflexible self-will, as distinct from passion; 3. Dry matter of fact or reality, as distinct from sentimentality or poetry" (12:188). We can see that Hazlitt's distinctions continue to be opposed to the modern style of intellect, with its emphasis on abstract reason, and we can see no less clearly that Hazlitt's definition of reason, as well as his understanding of moral sentiment, accord completely with Burke's view of human nature. We must resist, however, the temptation to regard Hazlitt as the proponent of the irrational, of undisciplined emotion and stupid sentimentality. For when Hazlitt talks about feeling he is in fact referring to man's affective nature and his tacit knowledge as the specific basis of all human thought and action. Reason, in Hazlitt's paradoxical view, does not precede but is the product of human feeling. Thus, he describes himself as "one of those who do not think that mankind are exactly governed by reason or a cool calculation of consequences. I rather believe that habit, imagination, sense, passion, prejudice, words make a strong and frequent diversion from the right line of prudence and wisdom" (17:275).

Such terms as habit, imagination, sense, passion, prejudice all fall into the general category of "feeling" as Hazlitt uses the term; reason alone does not answer to the needs of man's affective nature, for, as Hazlitt asserts, "In morals, as in philosophy, . . . what does not touch the heart, or come home to the feelings, goes comparatively for little or nothing" (12:50). Feeling functions as the equivalent of tacit knowledge—it is the basis of human thought and action—as we can see in Hazlitt's observation that "In art, in taste, in life, in speech, you decide from feeling, and not from reason; that is, from the impression of a number of things on the mind, which impression is true and well-founded, though you may not be able to analyse or account for it in the several particulars" (8:31). In other words, we decide from feeling in the sense that we cannot fully account for our actions and decisions on purely rational and demonstrable grounds; we know far more than we can tell; our actions always escape the grasp of our subsequent explanations. Accordingly, Hazlitt asserts that "common sense is tacit reason" (8:33)—tacit in the precise sense that it is a form of habitual thought that is not rationally explained, demonstrated, or justified—and he goes on to characterize conscience as "the same tacit sense of right and wrong" (8:33–34). The concept of tacit knowledge assumes the central importance of man's affective nature at the same time that it denies that we can provide rational justification for all our actions. Just as Hazlitt uses feeling as the equivalent of tacit knowing, so Burke's general idea of prejudice, which is also determined by man's affective nature, expresses the basic fact of tacit knowledge and recognizes the continuity of tradition as a basic vehicle of that knowledge.

Interestingly, as much as Hazlitt late in his life repudiated Burke's political influence, he clearly continued to see Burke's concept of prejudice as absolutely central to an understanding of human nature. In one of his last essays entitled "Paragraphs on Prejudice" (1830), Hazlitt considers the meaning and significance of prejudice, defined as "opinion or feeling, not for which there is no reason, but of which we cannot render a satisfactory account on the spot" (20:324). Arguing from the position of tacit knowledge, namely that "in all that we do, feel, or think, there is a leaven of *prejudice* (more or less extensive), *viz.*, something implied, of which we do not know or have forgotten the grounds" (20:326), Hazlitt forcefully establishes the fundamental distinction between what we know and what we can tell, between the more basic and extensive power of feeling as distinguished from the more limited range of abstract reason. Hazlitt writes:

The grounds of our opinions and tastes may be deep, and be scattered over a large surface; they may be various, remote and complicated, but the result will be sound and true, if they have existed at all, though we may not be able to analyse them into classes, or to recall the particular time, place, and circumstances of each individual case or branch of the evidence. The materials of thought and feeling, the body of facts and experience, are infinite, are constantly going on around us, and acting to produce an impression of good or evil, of assent or dissent to certain inferences; but to require that we should be prepared to retain the whole of this mass of experience in our memory, to resolve it into its component parts, and be able to quote chapter and verse for every conclusion we unavoidably draw from it, or else to discard the whole together as unworthy the attention of a rational being, is to betray an utter ignorance both of the limits and the several uses of the human capacity. The feeling of the truth of anything, or the soundness of the judgment formed upon it from repeated, actual impressions, is one thing: the power of vindicating and enforcing it, by distinctly appealing to or explaining those impressions, is another. (20:325)

In one sweeping move, Hazlitt dismisses the conventional distinction, and implied necessity of choosing, between reason and emotion, the abstract and the particular, the explicit and the implied, reform and tradition. Tacit knowing, which requires a proper understanding of Burke's idea of prejudice or Hazlitt's concept of feeling, involves an understanding of various levels of human experience. To dwell exclusively on any one level, which is characteristic of the modern style of intellect, is to diminish and impoverish our understanding of what it means to be a human being. Like human societies, human beings, according to Hazlitt, are best understood developmentally: that is, as moving through stages of expanding growth, awareness, and activity. But this process of expansion, which is most clearly revealed through the imagination, continually escapes and outpaces rational explanations and justifications. No single work expresses Hazlitt's awareness of the disjunction between the *"feeling* of the truth of anything" (tacit knowing) and the "power of vindicating and enforcing it" (rational explanation) than *The Spirit of the Age* (1825), to which we shall now turn.

Chapter Four
The Spirit of the Age

The Spirit of the Age, subtitled "Contemporary Portraits," exhibits some of Hazlitt's finest and most controversial writing. This volume of essays appeared early in 1825, with the following epigraph from *Hamlet:* "To know a man well, were to know himself." The book was also published in a Paris edition, and a second English edition was published in the same year (1825). Of the essays contained in *The Spirit of the Age,* the following were reprinted—some with additions and revisions—from earlier magazine articles: "Jeremy Bentham" (*New Monthly Magazine,* January 1824), "Rev. Mr. Irving" (*New Monthly Magazine,* February 1824), "Rev. Mr. Irving" (*New Monthly Magazine,* March 1824), "Sir Walter Scott" (*New Monthly Magazine,* April 1824), "Lord Eldon" (*New Monthly Magazine,* July 1824), "Mr. Canning" (*Examiner,* 11 July 1824), "Mr. Canning" (*Examiner,* 11 July 1824), and "Mr. Crabbe" (*London Magazine,* May 1821).

It is significant that Hazlitt should attach the epigraph from *Hamlet,* for *The Spirit of the Age* is a curious combination of criticism, description, and self-portraiture. The book combines Hazlitt's talent for characterizing others at the same time that he reveals his own opinions and idiosyncrasies. Thus, the apparent design of the work is not only to inform, summarize, and evaluate the accomplishments of Hazlitt's contemporaries, but also to express his mature understanding of the ethos—intellectual, political, literary—of his own time. Ian Jack is certainly right to observe that in *The Spirit of the Age* "Hazlitt was at once writing his spiritual autobiography and holding up a mirror to the age."[1]

One way to examine this important work is to focus on its key terms and multiple dimensions. Accordingly, we shall first look at Hazlitt's general use of the term "spirit of the age" and then consider the intellectual, political, and literary reverberations of Hazlitt's approach to his contemporaries.

"The Spirit of the Age"

We should initially realize that Hazlitt does not subscribe to the abstract idea of history as expressing a prevailing zeitgeist (loosely, "the spirit of the time or age"). Hazlitt does not entertain a sophisticated concept of history. He does, however, use the term "spirit of the age" as a kind of shorthand for characterizing what he regards as the prevailing tensions—intellectual, political, literary—of the period beginning with the French Revolution (1789) and running into the first quarter of the nineteenth century. Some of these tensions we have already looked at as Hazlitt takes issue, for example, with the modern philosophy. Now, in *The Spirit of the Age*, he tries to examine the many ramifications of this tension. Each author he discusses represents another variation and approach to the central issues of his time; Ian Jack has commented about Hazlitt's critical method in *The Spirit of the Age* that "It is not the individual book or poem that is the unit of consideration, but the writer himself."[2]

That Hazlitt understands the term "spirit of the age" as expressing a tension rather than a fixed position can be seen if we inspect his various uses of this term both within and outside *The Spirit of the Age*. In his essay "On the Pleasure of Hating" (1823), Hazlitt speaks of the spirit of the age as "the progress of intellectual refinement, warring with our natural infirmities" (12:128–29); and in an earlier *London Magazine* essay written in 1820 he observes: "In a word, literature and civilization have abstracted man from himself so far, that his existence is no longer *dramatic*. . . . If a bias to abstraction is evidently, then, the spirit of the age, dramatic poetry must be allowed to be most irreconcilable with this spirit; it is essentially individual and concrete, both in form and in power" (18:305).

From these two examples we can get a feel for how Hazlitt understands the "spirit of the age." The first example refers to a tension between the progress of intellect, meaning the tendency to develop and rely on ever-increasing abstraction (what we sometimes mean by "sophistication"), and the natural limitations that remind us of our individual defects and inherent fallibility. Hazlitt sees a significant conflict in his time between a heightened intellectual sophistication—represented especially by Godwin and Bentham, and to a lesser degree Coleridge—with its great emphasis on reason and method, and the basically affective nature of human beings—most powerfully represented by Burke and Sir Walter Scott—with its corresponding interest in feeling, tacit knowing, and "prejudice." The second example further clarifies this tension. Hazlitt asserts that the tension is evident both in "literature and civilization" and occurs between an increasing bias and reliance on "abstraction" and generalization, and a corresponding diminution of the dramatic and the individual. To use a contemporary term, Hazlitt sees the spirit of the age as involving a drift toward "depersonalization," which is reflected not only in an excessive reliance on reason (intellectually) and established authority (politically), but also in an equally excessive display of private emotion and self-aggrandizement (Byron, Wordsworth, and Coleridge are Hazlitt's favorite examples) that Hazlitt condemns as naked egotism. Hazlitt despises any poetry that resembles self-advertisement.

In *The Spirit of the Age* itself, Hazlitt's use of the term ranges from the casual or colloquial to the precise and relatively technical. About Rev. Edward Irving he casually observes: "He has revived exploded prejudices, he has scouted prevailing fashions. He has opposed the spirit of the age" (11:44). Here the term simply means Irving has resisted the major current of his time. Hazlitt says the same thing about his good friend Charles Lamb: "Mr. Lamb has succeeded not by conforming to *The Spirit of the Age*, but in opposition to it. He does not march boldly along with the crowd, but steals off the pavement to pick his way in the contrary direction. He prefers *bye-ways* to highways" (11:178). At the same time, in both the above examples and the following brief comparison of Sir Walter Scott and Lord Byron—"if the one [Scott] defers too much to the spirit of antiquity, the other [Byron] panders to the spirit of the age, goes to the very edge of extreme and licentious speculation" (11:76)—Hazlitt clearly uses the term to signify a clash between the past and the present. Thus we must recognize that the term can operate in two general ways. Used as a synonym for *contemporary*, the spirit of the age is opposed to the past and to a veneration of "antiquity." The term, however, also signifies and alludes to a major tension *within* the contemporary between the abstract and the dramatic, the speculative and the specific. The "spirit of the age," we shall now see, may best be viewed in three contexts: 1) the intellectual, reflecting an overreliance on reason at the expense of man's affective nature; 2) the political, which Hazlitt examines in light of the distinction between "Liberty" and "Legitimacy"; and 3) the literary, where the sympathetic imagination is threatened by a rising and dogmatic egotism.[3]

The Intellectual: Models of Mind

As we have seen in our earlier discussion of tacit knowing, Hazlitt is by no means an antirationalist, nor is he an unthinking sentimentalist. What he is quite suspicious of, though, is an excessive reliance on reason and empirical method to the detriment of man's affective nature. This increasing intellectual bias to abstraction, which Hazlitt treats as symptomatic of the spirit of the age, is seen most fully in his essays on Jeremy Bentham and William Godwin.

Hazlitt describes Bentham's influence as "purely intellectual" because he "devoted his life to the pursuit of abstract and general truths" (11:5). Because of Bentham's exclusive concern with facts and method, Hazlitt suggests that Bentham's principal interest, and central limitation, is that he submits facts "into his logical machinery and grind[s] them into the dust and powder of some subtle theory" (11:7). Treating man as purely a "logical animal" (11:8), Bentham ignores or is insensitive to man's feelings. His moral theory, based on the idea that man is essentially motivated by the desire to achieve pleasure and avoid pain, suffers from the basic flaw of all abstractions: He has "not made sufficient allowance for the varieties of human nature, and the caprices and irregularities of the human will" (11:8).

What Bentham has mistakenly done, and what Hazlitt treats as representative of the bias to abstraction symptomatic of the spirit of the age, is that Bentham has attempted to establish a wholly rational basis for understanding man's affective nature. In this effort, he has reduced human feeling to mere mechanism, human complexity to logical simplicity. Though Hazlitt happily concedes that the "laws of the affections are as necessary as those of optics," he goes on to notice, in response to Bentham's ignorance of man's affective nature, that "A calculation of consequences [a key concept of Bentham's Utilitarianism] is no more equivalent to a sentiment, than a *seriatim* enumeration of square yards or feet touches the fancy like the sight of the Alps or Andes" (11:9). In other words, Bentham has erroneously substituted a part—reason—for the whole—our affective life. Unlike Bentham, Hazlitt continually argues against any mechanistic model; where Bentham imposes a dichotomy between reason and feeling, Hazlitt sees tension and dialectic. Thus Hazlitt comments: "Our moral sentiments are made up of sympathies *and* antipathies, of sense *and* imagination, of understanding *and* prejudice" (11:8; emphasis added).

Initially, Godwin, too, leaned toward an "either/or" understanding

of the role of intellect in human nature. Like Bentham, Godwin subscribed to an abstract model of the human mind—a model he later
abandoned in his novels—ignoring or underestimating all those features that constitute tacit knowing. Hazlitt maintains that Godwin,
in his principal philosophical work, *Enquiry Concerning Political Justice*
(1793), "took abstract reason for the rule of conduct, and abstract good
for its end. He places the human mind on an elevation, from which it
commands a view of the whole line of moral consequences; and requires
it to conform its acts to the larger and more enlightened conscience
which it has thus acquired. He absolves man from the gross and narrow
ties of sense, custom, authority, private and local attachment, in order
that he may devote himself to the boundless pursuit of benevolence"
(11:18–19). In the last sentence of the above passage, we can see that
Godwin, like Bentham, has excluded all those "prejudices" tied to
man's affective nature: sense, custom, and private and local attachments. Subscribing to a definition of morals as *"reason without passion"*
(11:20), Godwin ironically performs a significant service by inadvertently revealing the fundamental weakness of his own, as well as Bentham's, position. Hazlitt perceptively writes: "if it is admitted that
Reason alone is not the sole and self-sufficient ground of morals, it is
to Mr. Godwin that we are indebted for having settled the point. . . .
His grand work is (at least) an *experimentum crucis* to show the weak
sides and imperfections of human reason as the sole law of human action" (11:23).

The models of mind presented by Bentham and Godwin are essentially philosophical. There is one other model of intellect, more literary
and political than philosophical, that deserves mention in this section.
It is a model that emerges from Hazlitt's comparison of the two most
important literary-political journals of his time, the conservative
Quarterly Review and the more liberal *Edinburgh Review,* for which Hazlitt wrote. Hazlitt's main point centers on the quality of mind that
characterizes the spirit of the age. In his view, the literary-political
opinions and discussions of the *Edinburgh Review* "are eminently characteristic of the Spirit of the Age; as it is the express object of the
Quarterly Review to discountenance and extinguish that spirit, both in
theory and practice" (11:127). For Hazlitt, what is representative
about the *Edinburgh Review* is that within its pages: "The principles
were by no means decidedly hostile to existing institutions: but the
spirit was that of fair and free discussion. . . . The *Edinburgh Review*
. . . asserts the supremacy of intellect: the pre-eminence it claims is

from an acknowledged superiority of talent and information and literary attainment, and it does not build one tittle of its influence on ignorance, or prejudice, or authority, or personal malevolence" (11:127–28).

In other words, the *Edinburgh Review* fully expresses and exemplifies the characteristic tension of the spirit of the age. It embodies Hazlitt's understanding of the spirit of the age as the free assertion of the power of mind. But, as we shall now see, many of the writers whom he discusses are preoccupied, like the *Quarterly Review,* with tying the mind (and imagination) to political power and prevailing opinion. Hazlitt analyses this phenomenon through one of his favorite distinctions—that between "Liberty" and "Legitimacy."

The Political: Liberty vs. Legitimacy

Hazlitt once asserted that the "love of liberty is the love of others; the love of power is the love of ourselves" (7:152). He treats the concept of liberty as having both a personal and political dimension. On the personal level, as we have seen, liberty is tied to free choice (philosophically) and to the power of imagination as a creative and moral attribute of mankind. On the political level, the concept of liberty presumes the highest regard for human initiative and our ability to act virtuously. The love of liberty, like the sympathetic imagination, is the love of others because it takes us out of ourselves, out of an egotistical preoccupation with self, and expresses our desire for others to exercise their free will on both a personal and political level.

The love of power, on the other hand, tends to diminish the value of the individual in defense of an abstraction of authority that Hazlitt calls "legitimacy." "Legitimacy" is not, as has been suggested (7:386), simply a synonym for Divine Right or royalist principles. Rather, Hazlitt uses the term as an all-purpose description of a slavish assertion of, and attachment to, power and the "right" of authority no matter what the circumstances. Legitimacy is *"a power above the law, and accountable only to heaven for its exercise, its use or its abuse"* (7:155). Moreover, on a broader scale, the love of power, or legitimacy, is the love of ourselves projected through some national abstraction—patriotism, tradition, authority—at the expense of recognizing the diverse experiences and persuasions of other individuals. Because legitimacy so often involves a form of exclusion, it invariably implies a contempt for others unlike ourselves, just as liberty encourages a respect for others.

Hazlitt sarcastically describes the "blessings of Legitimacy" as the use of "power restrained only by its own interests, follies, vices, and passions" (19:196). In light of legitimacy's preoccupation with preserving an abstraction called "power," along with its general disregard of individuals, it is not surprising that Hazlitt observes about monarchs: "There is but one question in the hearts of monarchs, whether mankind are their property or not" (12:122). Commenting on the French Revolution, and its aftermath, Hazlitt says, "In the late quarrel about Liberty, upwards of five millions of men have been killed, and *one king*" (20:140). The distinction between monarchs and men, kings and millions of individuals, points to the more basic tension of the spirit of the age between the abstract and the personal. As we shall see, Hazlitt employs the liberty/legitimacy distinction to identify the contrasting uses of imagination that characterize the spirit of the age. Those uses involve the exercise of imagination as either a tool of political power and entrenched authority or as an expression of intellectual, political, and creative freedom.

For instance, in his essays on Samuel Coleridge and Sir Walter Scott, he explicitly links the liberty/legitimacy distinction with the overall spirit of the age. In the former essay Hazlitt remarks:

> It was a misfortune to any man of talent to be born in the latter end of the last century. Genius stopped the way of Legitimacy. . . . The spirit of the monarchy was at variance with the spirit of the age. The flame of liberty, the light of intellect was to be extinguished with the sword—or with slander, whose edge is sharper than the sword. The war between power and reason was carried on. . . . The philosophers, the dry abstract reasoners, submitted to this reverse pretty well. . . . But the poets, the creatures of sympathy, could not stand the frowns both of king and people. (11:37)

We can follow Hazlitt's thought if we momentarily regather, strictly for analytic purposes, the diverse distinctions Hazlitt employs throughout *The Spirit of the Age*. Remembering that Hazlitt treats the concept of the spirit of the age as a tension, we can see that the key terms of that tension are as follows. On the one hand, there is an inclination, sometimes a hard and fast commitment, to abstraction, authority, legitimacy, and the use of the imagination as a political instrument. This, of course, is the tendency Hazlitt condemns. On the other, Hazlitt favors an opposed set of terms that emphasize the dramatic, the individual, liberty, and the free exercise of the imagination as an instrument of creative genius.

For example, when Hazlitt says that "Genius stopped the way of Legitimacy," he is alluding to several occurrences. Customarily, he uses "genius" to refer to the imagination as both a creative power and the expression of liberty—intellectual, political, literary—that is the outcome of unfettered imagination. Therefore, when genius stops the way of legitimacy, it means that imagination has become an instrument of political power, which is what Hazlitt believes happened to Coleridge. In Hazlitt's view, Coleridge, as well as others, could not withstand the tension of the spirit of the age and thus drifted toward the pole of legitimacy. In the war between "power and reason," power won out, particularly among the poets (according to Hazlitt) because they were most dependent on "sympathy" and most susceptible—if not servile— to the assurances of state authority. Clearly, Hazlitt is being controversial, polemic and possibly unfair; but he is not so doctrinaire that he is unable to apply the liberty/legitimacy distinction with considerable force and skill. This is particularly evident in his fascinating and sometimes misunderstood essay entitled "Sir Walter Scott."

Hazlitt's examination of Scott is highly reminiscent of his ambivalent response to Burke. There is no doubt in Hazlitt's mind that Scott is an extraordinary writer whose power, curiously, derives from the tension between Scott's unconscious and imaginative expression of liberty and his conscious commitment to the principles of legitimacy. On the one hand, Hazlitt writes that the "political bearing" of Scott's novels is "a relief to the mind, rarified as it has been with modern philosophy, and heated with ultra-radicalism" (11:65). Moreover, Scott is "a writer reconciling all the diversities of human nature to the reader. He does not enter into the distinctions of hostile sects or parties, but treats of the strength or the infirmity of the human mind, of the virtues or vices of the human breast, as they are to be found blended in the whole race of mankind" (11:65). Here we can see that Hazlitt praises Scott's ability to respect and express the sense of tension characteristic of the spirit of the age. Scott is at his best, Hazlitt argues, when he focuses on human nature, when he deals not with politics but with the complexity of human needs and desires.

And yet, on another level, Hazlitt argues that Scott is "besotted as to the moral of his own story" (11:65). That is, Scott's conscious political commitments to conservatism, authority, monarchy, and tradition in fact reveal the weaknesses, no less than the strengths, of his biases. His evident veneration of loyalty that is continually expressed in his novels is founded, as Hazlitt observes, "on *would-be* treason: he props the actual throne by the shadow of rebellion" (11:65). The essential honesty of Scott's imagination is at odds with his political leanings. Regarding the unconscious tension between Scott's imaginative understanding of human nature and his overt political biases, Hazlitt asks the question: "Is he infatuated enough, or does he so dote and drivel over his own slothful and self-willed prejudices, as to believe that he will make a single convert to the beauty of Legitimacy, that is, of lawless power and savage bigotry, when he himself is obliged to apologise for the horrors he describes, and even render his descriptions credible to the modern reader by referring to the authentic history of those delectable times?" (11:65).

In effect, Scott fully expresses the spirit of the age, even as he finally falls victim to his own need for legitimacy. The power of his imagination records the diversity of human nature and thus displays the basically affective nature of humanity. But he frequently turns his imagination into an instrument of political power and thereby undermines the strength of his literary vision. As Hazlitt says, "it is thus he administers charms and philtres to our love of Legitimacy, makes us conceive a horror of all reform, civil, political, or religious, and would fain put down the *Spirit of the Age*" (11:66).

If Scott's career dramatically reveals the tug of war between liberty and legitimacy, the power of imagination and the use of imagination as an extension of political power, Hazlitt's essay entitled "William Gifford" represents his sharpest and perhaps most vicious portrait of a person wholly committed to legitimacy. Because Gifford was the editor of the *Quarterly Review,* an extremely conservative, if not reactionary, journal, one would expect Hazlitt, given his political biases and his preference for the more liberal *Edinburgh Review,* to attack the editor of a rival publication. But the intensity and venom of Hazlitt's essay are not simply explained by personal animus. Hazlitt may caustically describe Gifford as a "happy combination of defects, natural and acquired" (11:114), but what most disturbs him is how Gifford represents a type of person who has completely "sold out" to legitimacy.

Although Hazlitt comments on Gifford's vanity and pedantry, it is his political subservience that he most strongly condemns. Earlier, in *A Letter to William Gifford, Esq.* (1819), Hazlitt set the tone for what he says in *The Spirit of the Age.* At that time, Hazlitt directly addressed

Gifford: "You are the *Government Critic,* a character nicely differing from that of a government spy—the invisible link that connects literature with the police" (9:13). Now Gifford is again attacked as a man who believes that "truth is to be weighed in the scales of opinion and prejudice; that power is equivalent to right" (11:115). Hazlitt then goes on to describe how Gifford strikingly exemplifies the principal features of legitimacy:

The character of his mind is an utter want of independence and magnanimity in all that he attempts. He cannot go alone. . . . He cannot conceive of anything different from what he finds it, and hates those who pretend to a greater reach of intellect or boldness of spirit than himself. He inclines, by a natural and deliberate bias, to the traditional in laws and government; to the orthodox in religion; to the safe in opinion; to the trite in imagination; to the technical in style; to whatever implies a surrender of individual judgment into the hands of authority, and a subjection of individual feeling to mechanic rules. (11:117)

Hazlitt's case against Gifford rises from the particular to the general, for it is Hazlitt's intention to show how Gifford's own loyalty to legitimacy embodies a general ideological position—that is, a predetermined pattern of attitudes and responses to literature, politics, and life in general. Thus Hazlitt composes a "character" of mind, rather than of the individual person alone. Gifford's mind is a specific example of legitimacy; he is a concrete example of a general condition. Such a condition of mind involves the repudiation of the following human attributes: independence, originality, uniqueness, nonconformity, and boldness. In effect, Hazlitt is saying that the mind of legitimacy stultifies the expression of liberty, both personal and political. Instead of respecting and nourishing the power of human imagination, Gifford debases that power by using it as an instrument of political expedience and subservience. Aligning himself with whatever is established in literature and politics (even if it is ineffective or decadent), Gifford, to an extent greater than any other figure in *The Spirit of the Age,* represents the absolute low point of Hazlitt's examination of the age. Like the character of his mind, the character of Gifford's journal, Hazlitt concludes, is "to pervert literature, from being the natural ally of freedom and humanity, into an engine of priestcraft and despotism, and to undermine the spirit of the English constitution and the independence of the English character" (11:124).

The Literary: The Sympathetic
Imagination versus Egotism

Comparing Lord Byron with Sir Walter Scott in his essay "Lord Byron," Hazlitt sets the tone and employs the key terms that characterize his literary estimation of the spirit of the age. Arguing that these two writers "afford a complete contrast to each other" (11:69), Hazlitt enumerates a series of distinctions that differentiate the sympathetic power of Scott's imagination from the egotistic nature of Byron's imagination. Byron, we are told, is "the creature of his own will . . . [who] exists not by sympathy, but by antipathy" (11:69). Hazlitt goes on to say that whatever Byron does "he must do in a more decided and daring manner than any one else. . . . Self-will, passion, the love of singularity, a disdain of himself and of others (with a conscious sense that this is among the ways and means of procuring admiration) are the proper categories of his mind: he is a lordly writer, is above his own reputation, and condescends to the muses with a scornful grace!" (11:70).

If Byron's principal object, reflective of his egotism, is to "display his own power, or vent his spleen, or astonish the reader," Scott's perhaps less spectacular but more imaginatively extensive goal is "to restore us to truth and nature" (11:70). Unlike Byron, whom Hazlitt calls "a pampered egotist" (11:77), Scott is far more expansive and generous. Where Byron "makes man after his own image," Scott "gives us man as he is, or as he was, in almost every variety of situation, action, and feeling" (11:71). In an incisive passage, Hazlitt describes how in Scott's fiction "the veil of egotism is rent":

He shows us the crowd of living men and women . . . and enriches our imaginations and relieves one passion by another, and expands and lightens reflection, and takes away that tightness at the breast which arises from thinking or wishing to think there is nothing in the world out of man's self!—In this point of view, [Scott] . . . is one of the greatest teachers of morality that ever lived, by emancipating the mind from petty, narrow, and bigotted prejudices: Lord Byron is the greatest pamperer of these prejudices . . . dogmatism and self-conceit. (11:71–72)

The point Hazlitt is making, and will establish again in his discussion of William Wordsworth, is that the imagination, freely exercised, emancipates the reader; yet many modern writers, including Byron and Wordsworth, turn their imaginative vision inward, imprisoning themselves, as Hazlitt says of Byron, within "the Bastile of his own ruling passions" (11:71).

Hazlitt's essay "Mr. Wordsworth" is a more complicated and controversial study of egotism than his examination of Byron. On first view, it seems surprising that Hazlitt would single out Wordsworth for criticism. After all, Wordsworth's poetry and poetic dogma are both strongly associated with the common people, purity and simplicity of feeling, and a powerful opposition to modern sophistication. Hazlitt begins his essay by claiming that "Mr. Wordsworth's genius is a pure emanation of the Spirit of the Age" (11:86); but he quickly concedes that Wordsworth "takes the simplest elements of nature and of the human mind, the mere abstract conditions inseparable from our being, and tries to compound a new system of poetry from them; and has perhaps succeeded as well as any one could" (11:86).

Nevertheless, Wordsworth's poetry is most representative and illuminating of the spirit of the age because "his poetry is founded on setting up an opposition (and pushing it to the utmost length) between the natural and the artificial; between the spirit of humanity, and the spirit of fashion and of the world" (11:87). What Hazlitt is getting at is that in defense of ordinary people and common feelings Wordsworth creates an abstraction of feeling and humanity, defending that abstraction as "natural" and rejecting all else as extraneous and "artificial." Hazlitt rejects such an oversimplification, even though it emanates from the very French Revolution he, on political grounds, admires. As much as Wordsworth's poetry "partakes of, and is carried along with, the revolutionary movement of our age" (11:87), it is at the same time a poetry that "levels" the imagination by imposing a political principle of equality on a mental faculty (the imagination) and literary form (poetry) that depend on genius, distinction, and discrimination.

Hazlitt thus catalogs the essential egotism behind Wordsworth's distinction between the natural and the artificial. He argues that Wordsworth's muse "proceeds on a principle of equality, and strives to reduce all things to the same standard. It is distinguished by a proud humility. It relies upon its own resources, and disdains external show and relief. . . . All the traditions of learning, all the superstitions of age, are obliterated and effaced. We begin *de novo,* on a *tabula rasa* of poetry" (11:87). In short, Wordsworth acts as if he is the sole and exclusive poetic voice of the "people," a position Hazlitt repudiates. Furthermore, Hazlitt is accusing Wordsworth, by beginning *"de novo,* on a *tabula rasa* of poetry," of either rejecting, or being completely ignorant of, the principle of tacit knowledge. Years earlier in his *Lectures on the English Poets* (1818), Hazlitt commented: "The great fault of a modern school of poetry is, that it is an experiment to reduce poetry to a mere effusion of natural sensibility; or what is worse, to divest it both of imaginary splendour and human passion, to surround the meanest objects with the morbid feelings and devouring egotism of the writers' own minds" (5:53).

Now we can see how much he has Wordsworth in mind as a dramatic example of the egotism inherent in the spirit of the age, an egotism that superimposes private dogma on personal feelings. In his essay "Character of Mr. Wordsworth's New Poem The Excursion" (*Examiner,* 21 and 28 August 1814), Hazlitt comments on "The Excursion": "The philosophical poet himself, perhaps, owes some of his love of nature to the opportunity it affords him of analyzing his own feelings, and contemplating his own powers,—of making every object about him a whole length mirror to reflect his favourite thoughts" (4:117). Two years later, Hazlitt returns to the same topic. In the guise of examining literary "Jacobinism," which he sees as "essentially at variance with the spirit of poetry," Hazlitt again singles out Wordsworth. Jacobinism, Hazlitt maintains, "levels all distinctions of art and nature: it has no pride, pomp, or circumstance belonging to it; it converts the whole principle of admiration in the poet (which is the essence of poetry) into admiration of himself" (7:144). Defining the spirit of Jacobin poetry. as "rank egotism," Hazlitt lists the Jacobin characteristics evident in Wordsworth's verse. Wordsworth, he argues, "tolerates nothing but what he himself creates. . . . He sees nothing but himself and the universe. He hates all greatness, and all pretension to it but his own. His egotism is in this respect a madness; for he scorns even the admiration of himself, thinking it a presumption in any one to suppose that he has taste or sense enough to understand him" (7:144).

Wordsworth is thus representative of the spirit of the age because he falsifies the tension between the abstract and the dramatic, the general and the individual, that represents the authentic spirit of the age. As Herschel Baker has correctly observed: "Wordsworth and Coleridge have a special place in [Hazlitt's] story not only because of their renown but because they epitomized for Hazlitt the failure of his age. In their progress—or decline—from reform to acquiescence in the *status quo* he read an allegory that haunted him for more than twenty years."[4] Wordsworth imposes a misleading distinction between the artificial and the natural, eventually opting for a highly limited and distorted version of feeling, mainly as a defense of his own poetic dogma. Much of what Wordsworth condemns as "artificial," Hazlitt, like Scott and Burke, venerates as expressive of "prejudice" and tacit knowledge. Much of what Wordsworth praises as "natural," Hazlitt rejects as an egotistical obsession, as a conspicuous failure of "communion with nature" that distinguishes the sympathetic imagination from modern egotism. Speaking of Wordsworth's negative response to Shakespeare, Hazlitt remarks, "We do not think our author [Wordsworth] has any very cordial sympathy with Shakespear. How should he? Shakespear was the least of an egotist of any body in the world" (11:92). Such a distinction between egotism and the imagination, as we shall next see, not only relates to Hazlitt's understanding of the spirit of the age, but also supports the basis of his aesthetic and literary views.

Chapter Five
Hazlitt on Art and Literature

Distinguishing between science and art, Hazlitt suggests that we "judge of science by the number of effects produced—of art by the energy which produces them. The one is knowledge—the other power" (18:8). Knowledge and power are certainly two key terms underlying Hazlitt's essays on art and literature. They are especially important in the basic distinction he establishes between the imaginative appeal of the arts and the verifiable results of the sciences. Hazlitt shares the view of his contemporary Thomas DeQuincey, who in distinguishing between a literature of knowledge and of power writes that "The function of the first is—to *teach;* the function of the second is—to *move. . . .* The first speaks to the *mere* discursive understanding; the second speaks ultimately, it may happen, to the higher understanding or reason, but always *through* affections of pleasure and sympathy."[1]

Unlike DeQuincey, however, Hazlitt does not distinguish between a literature of knowledge and of power because he identifies the sciences with the production of knowledge and imaginative literature with power. But he would certainly agree with DeQuincey that "there is a rarer thing than truth, namely, *power,* or deep sympathy with truth."[2] Hazlitt contends that the respective goals of science and of the arts are demonstrative truth and affective power. Poetry, as he says, "produces its effect by instantaneous sympathy" (5:15)—science by rational deliberation.

In order to understand the rationale informing Hazlitt's views of art and literature, we need to discuss his general view of the arts. Moreover, by examining Hazlitt's views of the arts we may have to revise a number of expectations associated with his political stands. Because Hazlitt was dedicated to the cause of political reform, it might seem reasonable to expect him to advocate a similarly progressive view of the arts. Yet, however much some of his contemporaries regard him as a knee-jerk ideologue whose responses are continually predictable, the fact is that Hazlitt entertains a complex and coherent view of the place and function of the arts in society.

In this chapter we shall concentrate on three interrelated areas that illumine Hazlitt's overall vision of the arts and literature: 1) his general distinction between the arts and sciences, most forcefully expressed in the essay "Why the Arts Are Not Progressive: A Fragment" (1814); 2) the corollary literary implications of this distinction in which he asserts the nonprogressive nature of imaginative literature and the poet's corresponding fall away from "nature"; and 3) the central importance of Shakespeare, whose imagination Hazlitt identifies with "the representative power of all nature" (5:70) and whose example defines the distinctive powers and possibilities of imaginative literature.

"Why the Arts Are Not Progressive"

To put it directly, the arts are not progressive because there is no evidence to suggest that the human imagination in its relation to nature is in any sense progressive—that is, susceptible to voluntary improvement and refinement. This may seem a peculiar, if not disappointing, contention in view of the current model of litearature that stresses the teaching of creative writing. Unlike many modern educators, Hazlitt does not believe the arts are an institution (hence his distrust of Sir Joshua Reynolds and the Royal Academy) or can be effectively taught through an institution.

The essay, "Why the Arts Are Not Progressive: A Fragment," originally appeared as two pieces—the first was entitled "Fragments on Art. 'Why the arts are not progressive'" (*Morning Chronicle*, 11 and 15 January 1814); the second piece was published as "Fine Arts. Whether they are Promoted by Academies and Public Institutions" (*Champion*, 11 September 1814). As Hazlitt observes, the idea that the arts are or can be progressive depends on a false analogy—namely that the arts will improve in the same way that scientific advances have occurred. Even so, the arts, which Hazlitt argues "depend on individual genius and incommunicable power" (4:161)—in other words, the power of genius and originality of art can neither be taught nor transferred—do not, like the sciences, proceed by empirical inquiry and experiment, nor do they produce knowledge subject to absolute demonstration. We do not ask a writer to prove the validity of a sonnet, nor should we ask a painter to demonstrate the factual content of a portrait or landscape. Since the arts, as Hazlitt maintains, "hold immediate communication with nature" (4:160)—that immediacy referring to the private relation between an artist and his experience of nature—they do not depend on empirical proof and independent confirmation. Similarly, when we respond to a poem or painting, we do not interpose standards of empirical proof and demonstration; we respond, as Hazlitt says, through "instantaneous sympathy." At best, we judge the arts on the basis of taste, which Hazlitt calls "the highest degree of sensibility, or the impression made on the most cultivated and sensible of minds," just as the arts themselves are the "result of the highest power both of feeling and invention" (4:164).

In Hazlitt's terms, the division between the fine arts, by which he means painting and poetry principally (4:161), and the sciences is *absolute,* in the sense that they depend on different procedures and require different responses to their distinctive truths. As Hazlitt puts it, "What is mechanical, reducible to rule, or capable of demonstration, is progressive, and admits of gradual improvement: what is not mechanical or definite, but depends on genius, taste, and feeling, very soon becomes stationary or retrograde, and loses more than it gains by transfusion" (4:161). Hazlitt's intention is not to assert the superiority of either the arts or sciences; it is his intention to sustain a fundamental distinction that, in his view, explains the characteristic progress of the one but not of the other. The sciences depend on a universally acknowledged method—that is, both a predictable way of setting up experiments and of confirming or invalidating results. Because this method is mechanical and reducible to rule, it lends itself to demonstration by any interested and technically competent outsider; the progress of the sciences depends on external confirmation and subsequent advancement or improvement of experimental results. Moreover, science is institutional; it is a community organized around common interests, procedures, and standards of proof.

The arts, on the other hand, are not institutional. Despite the presence of art schools, the most they can teach or improve is skill. They cannot teach originality or genius because the arts are fundamentally individualistic. Hazlitt's key terms—genius, taste, feeling—remind us of the basically affective nature of the arts. Because the arts rely on genius, taste, and feeling (normally, Hazlitt uses genius and feeling to refer to artistic invention and taste to refer to critical reception), their greatness always depends on individuals, not on the institutional enterprise of the scientific community. Artistic breakthroughs, unlike their scientific counterparts, do not necessarily lead to advances of any kind. Scientists can be educated—this is the root assumption of scientific method—and thus the sciences are progressive. Artists cannot be educated into creativity and genius because the arts do not have a method comparable to the sciences; hence the arts are not and cannot be progressive.

This observation alone leads Hazlitt to assert the additional claim that while the sciences have been characterized by steady advances, the arts, at least comparatively speaking, show a "stationary or retrogade" pattern. As Hazlitt puts it, "This is the peculiar distinction and privilege of each, of science and of art:—of the one, never to attain its utmost limit of perfection, and of the other, to arrive at it almost at once" (5:44–45). Hazlitt adopts this "nonprogressive" view of the arts based on at least three central observations. First, great artists have historically appeared sporadically; in fact, there is no historical evidence to suggest that great art has directly fostered, as distinguished from influenced, the emergence of additional great art. There is nothing predictable about the appearance of artistic originality in the way that one can assume further scientific advances. Indeed, Hazlitt delights in the paradox that much great art has emerged from comparatively barbarous societies—the point being that so-called advanced societies do not often (or necessarily) produce original art.

The second reason for Hazlitt's claiming the apparently "stationary or retrograde" nature of art deals with the relation between the artist and nature. Hazlitt earlier argued that the arts "hold immediate communication with nature" (4:160) and that "Nature is the soul of art. There is a strength in the imagination that reposes on nature, which nothing else can supply" (4:162). Hazlitt is intimating a complicated set of assumptions relating to his historical understanding of the imagination that will be discussed in the next section. Briefly, though, we can say that Hazlitt believes that historically the artist's relation to nature, both as the source and subject of art, has deteriorated. Hazlitt remarks: "Men at first produce effect by studying nature, and afterwards they look at nature only to produce effect" (6:248). This deterioration reaches its low point in artistic egotism—a point when the artist turns completely inward, using his imagination as a rival to, rather than a revealing of, the power of nature itself. In other words, the artist has interjected his own person—beliefs, opinions, idiosyncrasies—into his art as a substitute for or rival to the "immediate communication" between the imagination and nature.

Hazlitt's third reason for asserting the non-progressive nature of art has to do with the rise of literary criticism. As Hazlitt shrewdly observes, "The diffusion of taste is not the same thing as the improvement of taste; but it is only the former of these objects that is promoted by public institutions and other artificial means" (4:163). Hazlitt notices two phenomena occurring historically: taste, or generally an appreciation of the arts, becomes widespread but not greatly improved; and this occurrence is apparently related to the fact that as the number of great artists diminishes or remains at a standstill, the number of critics increases, in large part because of the needs of an artistic public. Criticism fills the gap left by the "stationary or retrograde" nature of artistic genius. Here Hazlitt clearly anticipates the recent argument of Walter Jackson Bate that "Whatever else can be said of the spate of critical writing that suddenly begins in the middle of the eighteenth century in England, we can describe it as an attempt . . . to reground the entire thinking about poetry in the light of one overwhelming fact: the obviously superior originality, and the at least apparently greater immediacy and universality of subject and appeal, of the poetry of earlier periods. The regrounding brought with it the fear . . . that literature and the other arts as well were threatened with inevitable decline."[3]

In his illuminating essay "The Periodical Press" (published in *Edinburgh Review*, May 1823), Hazlitt elaborates this position concisely: "We complain that this is a critical age; and that no great works of genius appear, because so much is said and written about them; while we ought to reverse the argument, and say, that it is because so many works of genius *have appeared* that they have left us little or nothing to do, but to think and talk about them" (16:212). Continuing the line of thought established in "Why the Arts are Not Progressive," Hazlitt further insists on a basic distinction between historical periods of artistic excellence and periods of social refinement. In addressing himself to the observed "anomaly in the history of the Fine Arts, that periods of the highest civilization are not usually distinguished by the greatest works of original genius" (16:212), Hazlitt sees that it is the nonprogressive nature of art that in itself prompts the advancement of "the most general refinement"; for it is these artistic models themselves that "by being generally studied, and diffused through social life, give birth to the last degrees of taste and civilization" (16:212). Criticism thus becomes an important function of civilization: It advances an understanding of the arts at the same time that it becomes an authoritative, which is not to say infallible, standard of artistic evaluation.

As I indicated in the beginning of this section, Hazlitt is certainly a political reformer and progressive; but his views of art and literature are not at all progressive or reformist. Again, this should not be viewed as an example of intellectual inconsistency; rather, it is another indication of Hazlitt's realistic assessment of the role of literature and the arts in society. Hazlitt has no sympathy for a democratization of the arts because he realizes that they depend on genius, taste, and feeling, not on one person and one vote, nor equal representation under the law. The authority of criticism, like the power of artistic genius, is individual and tacit, not institutional and explicit. Thus Hazlitt explains: "The principle of universal suffrage, however applicable to matters of government, which concern the common feelings and common interests of society, is by no means applicable to matters of taste, which can only be decided upon by the most refined understandings. The highest efforts of genius, in every walk of art, can never be properly understood by the generality of mankind. . . . The reputation ultimately, and often slowly affixed to works of genius is stamped upon them by authority, not by popular consent or the common sense of the world" (4:164).

In politics, as in his philosophical and moral views, Hazlitt strenuously defends the feelings, interests, and sense of common people. His political instincts are egalitarian; he is always opposed to political oppression. But as a critic and artist, he realizes that the nonprogressive nature of art is fundamentally different from either the progressive nature of the sciences or the reformist inclinations of democratic politics. Hazlitt advances such a view in his important essay entitled "Coriolanus," which first appeared in the *Examiner* (15 December 1816) and was later published in both *Characters of Shakespear's Plays* and *A View of the English Stage*. As he explains in this essay, poetry (like art generally) develops its own principles of authority, and these principles are not common but refined, not popular but elite. Like the imagination itself, the language of poetry "naturally falls in with the language of power. . . . The principle of poetry is a very anti-levelling principle. . . . It admits of no medium. It is every thing by excess" (4:214).

Poetry, Imagination, and Nature

Just as the arts in general are nonprogressive, relying on the expression and artistic "excess" of individual power, so imaginative literature follows a nonprogressive and, in Hazlitt's view, retrograde path. Why Hazlitt should adopt such a view can best be determined if we examine his basic assumptions concerning the relation of poetry, the imagination, and nature. The first place to turn is to Hazlitt's invaluable essay "On Poetry in General," which was first delivered as part of a series of public lectures at the Surrey Institution in January and February 1818. Some of these lectures were attended by the poet John Keats. In this essay Hazlitt defines poetry not as "a branch of authorship, but as "the universal language which the heart holds with nature and itself" (5:1–2). Poetry is not a role or a career but a relation with nature expressed solely through "the language of the imagination." Hazlitt goes on to define the imagination as "that faculty which represents objects, not as they are in themselves, but as they are moulded by other thoughts and feelings, into an infinite variety of shapes and combinations of power" (5:3). Because the language of poetry is the expression of the relation between imagination and nature, it operates most powerfully on a tacit level. That is, poetry is most effective when it is least conscious of itself. As much as the imagination is "the power of feigning things according to nature" (5:46), as Hazlitt argues in his lecture "On Shakespeare and Milton," the power of invention is largely immediate and involuntary, not distanced and deliberate. Similarly, in his lecture "On the English Novelists," Hazlitt insists that "this intuitive perception of the hidden analogies of things, or, as it may be called, this instinct of *the imagination,* is, perhaps, what stamps the character of genius on the productions of art more than any other circumstance: for it works unconsciously, like nature, and receives its impression from a kind of inspiration" (6:109).

Although "inspiration" is a vague term, Hazlitt simply uses it to distinguish the nonprogressive relation of imagination and nature from the progressive and deliberate results of the sciences. Hazlitt is most insistent about the unconscious expressions of artistic genius because he regards the poet as the medium—not the manipulator—through whom the imagination communicates with nature. This may make poetry sound like a seance, but there is no doubt that Hazlitt believes poetry to be a universal language spoken, paradoxically, only by the few. To use Hazlitt's analogy, the instinct of the imagination is like nature because both are unconscious forces. Precisely when the artist becomes consciously manipulative of his imagination is the point at which Hazlitt sees the decline of poetry; for he believes, as he states in his lecture "On the Living Poets," that the "love of nature is the first thing in the mind of the true poet: the admiration of himself the last" (5:144–45).

In Hazlitt's view, the decline of the arts occurs when poets present themselves as artists and express, not their basically unconscious relation with nature, but their self-conscious response to nature. Historically, Hazlitt sees this decline, which is by no means irreversible, occurring shortly after the Elizabethan Age. In his lecture "On Dryden and Pope," Hazlitt uses terms to describe this decline that clearly emphasize a rising self-consciousness: "poetry had . . . in general declined, by successive gradations, from the poetry of imagination, in the time of Elizabeth, to the poetry of fancy . . . in the time of Charles I . . . to that of wit, as in the reign of Charles II and Queen Anne. It degenerated into the poetry of mere common places, both in style and thought, in the succeeding reigns" (5:82–83). Imagination, fancy, wit, the commonplace: Such an alleged erosion represents a fall from immediacy with nature, a decline in the language of poetry from the unconscious to an increasing self-consciousness, and a corresponding diminishment of the elevated vision associated with imaginative expression. The phenomenon Hazlitt observes has been recently described by Walter Jackson Bate, who argues "that the remorseless deepening of self-consciousness, before the rich and intimidating legacy of the past, has become the greatest single problem . . . [of] modern art."[4]

In his lecture "On the Dramatic Writers Contemporary with Shakespear," Hazlitt compares the Elizabethan dramatists with two of their successors, Beaumont and Fletcher, and says of the Elizabethans that "It is the reality of things present to their imaginations, that makes these writers so fine. . . . Nature lies open to them like a book, and was not to them 'invisible, or dimly seen' through a veil of words and filmy abstractions" (6:212–13). Here Hazlitt emphasizes the immediacy of the Elizabethan's relation to nature, the sense in which these dramatists were the medium through whom nature spoke. But, according to Hazlitt, Beaumont and Fletcher lacked this relation with nature and only saw nature through a "veil of words and filmy abstractions." Their language, he observes in his lecture "On Beaumont and Fletcher," was self-conscious, manipulatory, and artificial: "Beaumont and Fletcher were the first . . . who laid the foundation of the artificial diction and tinselled pomp of the next generation of poets, by aiming at a profusion of ambitious ornaments, and by translating the commonest circumstances into the language of metaphor and passion"

(6:250–51). Later Hazlitt refers to Beaumont and Fletcher's "misplaced and inordinate craving after striking effect and continual excitement." What he is thinking of is their substitution—or, as he says, "translation"—of a contrived language of "metaphor and passion" for an authentic expression of the relation between the poet, imagination, and nature.

Nevertheless, this process of poetic decline is not irreversible. Since the arts depend on genius, taste, and feeling, there is nothing to prevent an original artist from appearing at the most improbable moment. This argument is a corollary to the concept of the nonprogressive nature of art. But, given Hazlitt's argument that the arts have historically declined in general, it is true to say that original artists will, over the course of history, encounter greater obstacles to the expression of their creativity. For one thing, so-called advanced societies will prefer art that reflects or expresses their values; that is, an increasing self-consciousness and sophistication, which are principal attributes of civilization, will make a poet's immediate relation with nature less likely to occur because these two attributes require distance rather than immediacy. Still, Hazlitt suggests a way, however difficult, to resist this process of decline. In his introductory lecture to *The Dramatic Literature of the Age of Elizabeth,* he writes:

The first impulse of genius is to create what never existed before: the contemplation of that, which is so created, is sufficient to satisfy the demands of taste; and it is the habitual study and imitation of the original models that takes away the power, and even wish to do the like. Taste limps after genius, and from copying the artificial models, we lose sight of the living principle of nature. It is the effort we make, and the impulse we acquire, in overcoming the first obstacles, that projects us forward; it is the necessity for exertion that makes us conscious of our strength. (6:187)

To the question, as Walter Jackson Bate puts it, "*What is there left to do?*"[5] Hazlitt responds: Above all do not imitate, for imitation rapidly becomes intimidation. This is the reason that the concept of originality developed in the late eighteenth century, for this concept represents an assertion of freedom from the intimidating presence of past literary accomplishments. At no previous time in English literature were authors so aware of the art that preceded them. Thus Hazlitt, in counseling against imitation—by which he means depending on past literary models and assuming that genius is an acquired skill—emphasizes the importance of "effort," "exertion," and "strength." Art requires efforts of imagination, not acts of will. Although the goal of all art remains what Hazlitt calls "the living principle of nature," the results of that pursuit—artistically speaking—must change as previous forms of art become exhausted. Both the design and effect of past art may be used up, largely because of the fact that the arts are in competition with one another. As Hazlitt observes, "literature is confined not only within certain *natural,* but also within *local* and *temporary* limits, which necessarily have fewer available topics; and when these are exhausted, it becomes a *caput mortuum,* a shadow of itself. . . . Farther, the fine arts, by their spread, interfere with one another, and hinder the growth of originality" (16:216).

Hazlitt explains his distinction between "natural" and "local" or "temporary" limits when he contends that "not only are literature and art circumscribed by the limits of the nature of the mind of man, but each age or nation has a standard of its own. . . . Popularity can only be insured by the sympathy of the audience with any given mode of representing nature" (16:215–16). Significantly, these observations appear in an essay entitled "The Periodical Press" (1823). As we shall see in the next chapter, the periodical writers of the early eighteenth century represent a new mode of literature, one adjusted to the decline of poetry, and they are viewed by Hazlitt as the forerunners of another new mode of representing nature that would, in some ways, displace poetry: the novel. But the essential point for now is Hazlitt's awareness of what in the present day has been called "the anxiety of influence," the intimidating presence and effects of strong literary precursors.[6]

Let us summarize the implications of Hazlitt's position regarding the nonprogressive nature of literature. First, the imagination joins man most immediately with nature; it is the faculty of mind by which man invents according to nature. Like nature, it operates most forcefully on an unconscious level. Poetry is the language that most fully expresses the relation between man and nature.[7] Historically as man gains distance from and develops perspectives of nature, it happens that reason, detachment and sophistication gradually displace a poetic (or imaginative) relation between man and nature. Although this process of change and detachment is not irreversible, it certainly impedes man's poetic relation to nature in two basic ways. With the rise of reason, a self-conscious perspective of and response to nature is encouraged. Correspondingly, our experience of nature is altered from one of immediacy to one of distance and detachment and poets themselves become increasingly conscious of occupying the role of poet rather than simply being poets. In turn, the language of poetry deteriorates from the spontaneously imaginative to the carefully contrived. The poet's function shifts from being that of a medium through whom nature speaks to that of a manipulator of nature; the poet's ego displaces the experience of nature, a process Hazlitt describes as follows: "Men at first produce effect by studying nature, and afterwards they look at nature only to produce effect" (6:248).

Historically, then, man's relation with nature has altered, and that alteration is most conspicuous in the language of poetry. What has been good for the sciences and produced progress—the rise of reason, empiricism, and the experimental method—has inadvertently undermined the prospects of poetry. Science relies on an ability to abstract oneself from nature; poetry relies on a relationship of immediacy with nature. Still, if poetry is on the decline, Hazlitt is wise enough to see that other forms of literature may evolve from an altered relation with nature. Art can adapt to new realities. In his lecture "On Dryden and Pope," Hazlitt realizes that although poetry declined in the eighteenth century—so much so that he describes its greatest poet, Alexander Pope, as having a mind that was "the antithesis of strength and grandeur; its power was the power of indifference" (5:70–71)—its rapid decline also heralded the rise of the novel. If Pope had "none of the enthusiasm of poetry" and "was in poetry what the sceptic is in religion" (5:70–71), he was so because, as Hazlitt argues, he adopted and imitated exhausted literary models.

Yet at such a time of poetic decline a number of periodical writers, as well as such novelists as Defoe, Fielding, and Richardson, adjusted to the conditions of the time and exerted a strength of imagination through a new form of literature, the novel, which represents a new relation between man and nature. Charles I. Patterson, Jr., has argued that Hazlitt presents "the first clear and well-defined conception of fiction from a great English critic."[8] A more accurate statement would be to say that Hazlitt probably offers the first rigorous conception of realistic or mimetic (as opposed to ideal or moral) fiction. On the other hand, Patterson is correct to say that for Hazlitt fiction "provides an escape, but an escape *into* the world, not away from it."

Of the novel, Hazlitt comments, "If poetry has 'something more divine in it,' this savours more of humanity" (6:106). In other words, the novel is a new form of literature accommodated to the decline of poetry; it represents a shift away from the grander vision of poetry, particularly the epic and tragedy, to the more mundane but humane experience of ordinary people living in an urban and commercial society. As Hazlitt sees it, the principal vision of the novel involves a new social and psychological aspect of nature:

We find there [in the novel] a close imitation of men and manners; we see the very web and texture of society as it really exists, and as we meet with it when we come into the world. . . . We are brought acquainted with the motives and characters of mankind, imbibe our notions of virtue and vice from practical examples, and are taught a knowledge of the world. . . . Extremes are said to meet: and the works of imagination, as they are called, sometimes come the nearest to truth and nature. . . . The painter of manners gives the facts of human nature, and leaves us to draw the inference. (6:106–107)

Ultimately, what distinguishes the novel from poetry is its greater "realism"—that is, its closer imitation of social and psychological behavior. As Hazlitt recognizes, an urban and commercial society requires a form of literature that expresses its needs and interests in a more powerful and public way than the essentially private and elevated vision of poetry could convey. To a degree, the novel substitutes knowledge for imaginative power; it teaches its readers about men and manners, the structure of society, the behavior of individuals, and even establishes a practical basis for our understanding of vice and virtue. The novel teaches not by imitating other forms of literature but by imitating other patterns of life.

Formulating his observation paradoxically, Hazlitt argues that the alleged "extremes" of imagination, as distinguished from "truth" and "nature," in fact meet in the realism of many eighteenth-century novels. It requires strength of imagination to be realistic, no less than to be sublime. Comparing the eighteenth-century novelist Henry Fielding with Shakespeare, Hazlitt remarks: "As a mere observer of human nature, [Fielding] was little inferior to Shakespeare, though without any of the genius and poetic qualities of his mind" (6:113). But if Fielding's realism lacks "poetic qualities"—and it is deliberately designed to do so—it has other compensating imaginative strengths, which Hazlitt describes as follows: "The extreme subtlety of observation on the springs of human conduct in ordinary characters, is only equalled by the ingenuity of contrivance in bringing those springs into play. . . . The detection is always complete, and made with the certainty and skill of a philosophical experiment, and the obviousness and familiarity of a casual observation. . . . The feeling of the general principles of human nature operating in particular circumstances, is always intense, and uppermost in his mind; and he makes use of incident and situation only to bring out character" (6:113).

The comparison of Fielding with Shakespeare is especially apt because it points to the role Shakespeare plays in Hazlitt's understanding of English literary history. For Hazlitt, Shakespeare represents the high point of English poetry; the reasons for this view we shall examine shortly. The novel, as we have seen, follows the decline of poetry in the eighteenth century. Yet, as the novel—represented by Henry Fielding in this case—succeeds poetry as the most popular form of literature, that very tradition of the realistic novel evolves, to a large extent, from the author whose poetic vision it supposedly displaces: Shakespeare. When Hazlitt praises Fielding's use of character and commends his effective portrayal of the "feeling of the general principles of human nature operating in particular circumstances," he is pointing to how Fielding not only succeeds Shakespeare the poet but also continues the tradition of Shakespeare the realistic dramatist. The continued impact of Shakespeare's influence should not be surprising if we recognize that in Hazlitt's understanding of English literature all roads return to Shakespeare. Why this is so we shall now examine.

William Shakespeare

As a literary critic, Hazlitt is much more interested in what literature is and does than in what it means. For the most part, therefore, he does not write practical criticism, which is to say he rarely explicates a literary passage or work. But neither is Hazlitt a theoretical critic; he consistently resists the tendency toward abstraction so representative of his age. If labels are necessary, Hazlitt is best described as an "expressionistic"—not an impressionistic—critic. That is, he identifies with the author's process of creation rather than with the impression left by the text itself. Hazlitt practices and promotes a creative understanding of how the imagination expresses itself *through* art and literature. Roy Park has accurately said that Hazlitt "was the most consistent and articulate advocate of the experiential response in the early nineteenth century."[9]

Because of his overriding interest in what literature is and how it appeals to and affects the audience, Hazlitt writes about literature from the point of view of one who creates literature. Thus, the most marked characteristics of his criticism are its ability to convey an inside view of an artist's vision and its sensitivity, especially to the universal appeal of strong literature. The strength and power of literature are key terms because Hazlitt assumes that "the greatest strength of genius is shewn in describing the strongest passions: for the power of the imagination, in works of invention, must be in proportion to the force of the natural impressions, which are the subject of them" (4:271).

Stated another way, Hazlitt examines the distinctive power of literature not by describing or explaining a literary passage or work, but by expressing its principal effects. Although this mode of criticism has sometimes been repudiated as "impressionistic," when Hazlitt is at his best, which is often, he achieves a strength similar to that which he attributes to Shakespeare on stage: "The only way in which Shakespeare appears to greater advantage on the stage than common writers is, that he stimulates the faculties . . . more" (5:222). Hazlitt, too, stimulates his readers by attending to the distinctive "feel" or experience of a literary work and to how that experience embodies the power of a literary imagination.

Having looked at Hazlitt's general view of the nonprogressive nature of the arts and literature, it is time to focus exclusively on his views of Shakespeare. Hazlitt's observations on Shakespeare are collected in his volume *Characters of Shakespear's Plays* (1817) and dotted throughout his *Lectures on the English Poets* (1818) and *A View of the English Stage* (1818), the latter volume dealing with actual stage productions. Hazlitt's comments tell us as much about his responses to literature as they do about Shakespeare's drama. This is hardly surprising, if we recall that in the history of literary criticism since the Elizabethan Age examinations of Shakespeare have consistently reflected the predominant tastes and literary preoccupations of the time during which a particular critic was writing. That Hazlitt's criticism of Shakespeare should be much concerned with imagination and character reflects Hazlitt's larger desire to defend the power of imagination in response to an overreliance on reason and to assert the importance of character as a concrete and dramatic expression of the power of imagination. Hazlitt consistently maintains that the "concrete, and not the abstract, is the object of painting, and of all the works of imagination" (18:78); nothing in his mind is more concrete than Shakespeare's dramatic imagination.

To approach and assess Hazlitt's understanding of Shakespeare, we must first sort Hazlitt's basic assumptions and interests. For example, when Hazlitt talks about Shakespeare he rarely looks at his works as drama. Rather, he approaches the plays as a reader (not a spectator), cheerfully admitting that he "does not like to see our author's plays acted" (4:236). There are several reasons why he approaches Shakespeare's plays as books. In his essay on *A Midsummer Night's Dream*, Hazlitt compares the audience of a play with the reader of a book and remarks: "Poetry and the stage do not agree well together. . . . The *ideal* can have no place upon the stage, which is a picture without perspective; everything there is in the foreground. . . . Where all is left to the imagination (as is the case in reading) every circumstance, near or remote, has an equal chance of being kept in mind, and tells according to the mixed impression of all that has been suggested. But the imagination cannot sufficiently qualify the actual impressions of the senses. . . . The boards of a theatre and the regions of fancy are not the same thing" (4:247–48).

Hazlitt clearly assumes that any stage production, however effective, inhibits the spectator's imagination by presenting itself as a substitute for the text. The representation of the stage necessarily limits the experience of a reader. In Hazlitt's view, the text is both primary and, in a positive sense, indeterminate; a stage production is secondary, both because it is a substitute and because it leaves little to the imagination and its "ideal" constructs. Because a stage production attempts to do the work for the audience, Hazlitt thinks of the stage as all foreground; a particular production crowds out or contains the spectator's imagination, whereas a reader of a text can cast, costume, and produce any number of productions within his imagination. Since Hazlitt is such a committed *reader* of Shakespeare, his interests are critical, not theatrical. Thus, he contends that the "stage is not in general the best place to study our author's characters in" (4:324). As much emphasis should be put on the word *study* as on *characters*.

In the strictest sense, Hazlitt is a student of Shakespeare. He regards Shakespeare as the shrewdest student of life, which is what Hazlitt means by "nature." In his essay on *Macbeth*, Hazlitt comments that Shakespeare's "genius alone appeared to possess the resources of nature. . . . His plays have the force of things upon the mind" (4:186). Similarly, in his essay "Mr. Kean's Macbeth," Hazlitt continues: "If to *invent according to nature,* be the true definition of genius, Shakespear had more of this quality than any other writer. He might be said to have been a joint-worker with Nature, and to have created an imaginary world of his own, which has all the appearance and truth of reality. . . . It is the business of poetry, and indeed of all works of imagination, to exhibit the species through the individual. Otherwise, there can be no opportunity for the exercise of the imagination" (5:204).

The central questions to ask here are, what does Hazlitt mean by "resources of nature" and why does he credit Shakespeare with having these "resources." The questions may be addressed in several ways. First, Hazlitt treats Shakespeare as the preeminent English poet before the "fall" away from nature. Like the force of nature, Shakespeare's imagination expresses the power of the unconscious, as distinguished from the egotism that Hazlitt associates with self-consciousness. Moreover, Shakespeare was not intimidated by strong literary precursors. In an essay entitled "On Posthumous Fame" (1814) Hazlitt attributes Shakespeare's lack of "anxiety" to the fact that "he was almost entirely a man of genius; . . . he was either not intimately conversant with the productions of the great writers who had gone before him, or at least was not much indebted to them: he revelled in the world of observation and of fancy. . . . His mind was of too prolific and active a kind to dwell . . . [on] the genius of others' (4:23). As one recent critic has said: "Shakespeare belongs to the giant age before the flood, before the anxiety of influence became central to poetic consciousness."[10] Shakespeare was not a self-conscious poet preoccupied with his "role" and place in literary history; he was a dramatist who wrote to entertain audiences, not to impress critics or chase after fame. As a "joint-worker with Nature," Shakespeare created an imaginary world with real people in it.

Because Shakespeare's imagination was at once so receptive and expressive, it conveys a sense of reality—of correspondence to human experience—in two distinct and interrelated ways. For example, when Hazlitt comments that Shakespeare's plays have "the force of things upon the mind," he is suggesting that Shakespeare has so reduced the distance between man and nature, as well as that between audience and drama, that we *feel* his plays to be an immediate and authentic experience.[11] We do not feel that we are spectators of drama, so much as

participants in life. The principal way Shakespeare achieves this effect
is through his representation of character. By exhibiting, as Hazlitt
says,"the species through the individual"—that is, the power and complexity of human nature through the use of character—Shakespeare
attracts our imagination and sympathy. Hazlitt's best known work on
Shakespeare is entitled *Characters of Shakespear's Plays,* so it is only appropriate that we carefully examine what Hazlitt means by character
and how character serves as Shakespeare's principal vehicle for expressing nature.

Hazlitt credits Shakespeare with a "profound knowledge of character" (4:195). The nature of that profundity involves some different and
perhaps unique views of what makes a "character" in imaginative literature. For example, one of the ways Shakespeare's imagination expresses "the species through the individual" reveals a unique facet of
Shakespeare's mind—what Hazlitt calls "its generic quality, its power
of communication with all other minds." In his lecture "On Shakespeare and Milton," Hazlitt continues, saying that Shakespeare's mind
"contained a universe of thought and feeling within itself, and had no
one peculiar bias, or exclusive excellence more than another. . . . He
was the least of an egotist that it was possible to be. He was nothing
in himself; but he was all that others were, or that they could become"
(5:47). Because Shakespeare was "the least of an egotist"—that is, not
preoccupied with parading his own poetic presence—he was most able
to express his experience of the broadest range of characters. His lack
of self-consciousness enabled him to dramatize the unique identities—
actions, emotions, thought processes—of many other kinds of people.
Shakespeare's lack of egotism allowed him to conceive of character not
simply socially or even emotionally and mentally, but perceptually.
When Shakespeare imagined a character, as Hazlitt remarks, "he not
only entered into all its thoughts and feelings, but seemed instantly
. . . to be surrounded with all the same objects" (5:48). Through
Shakespeare's characters we not only think what they think, feel what
they feel, but also, most remarkably, see as they see.

Hazlitt's understanding of Shakespeare's characters thus involves
three levels of characterization: social identity, mental behavior, and
perceptual outlook. An example of the first level of characterization
can be seen in Hazlitt's observation on *Othello* that "The picturesque
contrasts of character . . . are almost as remarkable as the depth of
passion. The Moor Othello, the gentle Desdemona, the villain Iago,

the good-natured Cassio, the fool Roderigo, present a range and variety of character" (4:200). When Hazlitt discusses Lady Macbeth, he clearly focuses on motivation and mental behavior; he writes, "Her fault seems to have been an excess of that strong principle of self-interest and family aggrandisement, not amenable to the common feelings of compassion and justice, which is so marked a feature in barbarous nations and times" (4:189). The perceptual level of character is more subtle because it serves as a backdrop for how characters interpret events and other people. Thinking of the good intentions of a character like Brutus in *Julius Caesar,* Hazlitt observes: "Those who mean well themselves think well of others, and fall a prey to their security" (4:198); or about Hamlet, Hazlitt comments that he "is not a character marked by strength of will or even of passion, but by refinement of thought and sentiment" (4:233).

To these levels of character Hazlitt adds an additional attribute of character: the character's moral identity. Because Hazlitt believes Shakespeare to be the "master of the mixed motives of human character" (4:236), he recognizes that Shakespeare's imagination is such that it displays, but does not denounce, human actions of all kinds. Praising Shakespeare's "wonderful truth and individuality of conception" (5:50), Hazlitt likens Shakespeare to a "ventriloquist [who] throws his imagination out of himself, and makes every word appear to proceed from the mouth of the person in whose name it is given" (5:50). This act of ventriloquism has moral consequences that reveal Hazlitt's basic views of the general function of character and the imagination. Simply put, Hazlitt exempts Shakespeare's imagination from any moral responsibility. When he says, in his examination of *Troilus and Cressida,* that Shakespeare's genius was "dramatic" (4:225), he is thinking less of drama per se than of Shakespeare's peculiar handling of character and the consequences of their actions. Hazlitt asserts that Shakespeare "saw both sides of a question, the different views taken of it according to the different interests of the parties concerned. . . . He was at once an actor and spectator in the scene" (4:225). To be at once an actor and spectator, however, and to avoid taking sides, may heighten our sense of reality, but it also can lower our moral expectations. Perhaps recalling Samuel Johnson's accusation that Shakespeare often sacrificed virtue for convenience,[12] Hazlitt fully realizes the moral (or amoral) implications of this position, as they apply not only to Shakespeare specifically but also to the use of the imagination in general.

In his discussion of *Measure for Measure,* Hazlitt establishes the fundamental position that "Shakespear was in one sense the least moral of all writers; for morality (commonly so called) is made up of antipathies; and his talent consisted in sympathy with human nature. . . . In one sense, Shakespear was no moralist at all; in another, he was the greatest of all moralists. He was a moralist in the same sense in which nature is one. . . . He shewed the greatest knowledge of humanity with the greatest fellow-feeling for it" (4:346–47). Here we can see most clearly—because Hazlitt states so succinctly—how Shakespeare embodies the powers and possibilities of the imagination. To begin with, Hazlitt assumes a distinction between moral judgment, and moral knowledge and power. Ordinarily, morality does involve "antipathies," which are a consequence of distinguishing between what is right and wrong, or good and evil. But the imagination, as Hazlitt sees it, expresses itself through "sympathy with human nature"—through, that is, a temporary suspension of judgment so that the power of feeling and understanding can be fully realized. In strong literature, an imaginative grasp and sympathy with human nature supersede the impulse to judge morally. Thus Hazlitt sees that one of Shakespeare's most evil characters, Iago in *Othello,* is "a complete abstraction of the intellectual from the moral being" (5:215); he is one of those characters "whose heads are as acute and active as their hearts are hard and callous" (4:206). But Hazlitt also realizes that the character of Iago enables Shakespeare to express the more comprehensive moral knowledge "that the love of power, which is another name for the love of mischief, is natural to man" (4:206)—that is, common to human nature.

If Shakespeare's imagination does not exercise moral judgment, it does express moral power and understanding. This, for Hazlitt, is the most valuable and humane contribution that Shakespeare (and literature generally) may make. Hazlitt praises Shakespeare's "pervading comprehensive power" (4:228). That power is seen in the third act of *Othello,* which Hazlitt says is Shakespeare's "finest display, not of knowledge or passion separately, but of the two combined, of the knowledge of character with the expression of passion" (4:202). Shakespeare, says Hazlitt, is the master "of the connecting links of the passions and their effect upon the mind" (4:206).

Clearly, knowledge and passion, character and expression, are key elements in Hazlitt's praise of Shakespeare's imagination. What makes that imagination exemplary—the model for subsequent literature—is its ability to combine and connect the elements of drama with the essentials of humanity, or what Hazlitt calls a profound knowledge with intense "fellow-feeling." Above all, Shakespeare's unique gift was his lack of desire to be unique, his unwillingness to focus on his own ego. As Hazlitt says in his lecture "On Shakespeare and Milton," Shakespeare "was just like any other man, but that he was like all other men" (5:47). Shakespeare was, paradoxically, the greatest poet by virtue of being, through his imagination, the most common man.

Chapter Six

The Author, the Man, and the Essay

Herschel Baker has commented that Hazlitt's "subject is himself."[1] It is true that for an author who was so stridently opposed to egotism, Hazlitt writes a great deal about himself and his opinions. This certainly appears to be a contradiction, or, as Hazlitt was fond of saying, a "paradox." The paradox, however, is easily explained once we see that Hazlitt, most strongly and vividly in his essays, attacked the common—and, in his view, spurious—distinction between the author and the man. In his essay "On the Periodical Essayists," Hazlitt speaks of Montaigne as "the father of . . . personal authorship" (6:95); he further argues that "The great merit of Montaigne then was, that he may be said to have been the first who had the courage to say as an author what he felt as a man" (6:92).

To understand how Hazlitt, as an author, uses himself and his experiences and how he judges others who write essays, we need to examine his general idea of "personal authorship" and how, at its best, it requires the "courage to say as an author what [is] felt as a man." Of the essay form, Hazlitt maintains that "It is in morals and manners what the experimental is in natural philosophy, as opposed to the dogmatical method" (6:91). Here Hazlitt reveals two specific attributes of the essay form: First, its chief topics are morals and manners, but only as they apply to everyday experiences. These topics, however, must not be treated as abstractions. Thus Hazlitt likens the method of the essay with an "experimental," rather than "dogmatical" approach—by which he means that the essay proceeds from specifics, from common occurrences, and it moves to tentative rather than conclusive positions. The method of essay writing is also "experimental" in the sense that it is a form of writing that continually undergoes refinements, revisions, readjustments: Its form and content are similarly open-ended.[2]

Hazlitt further contends that "The writers I speak of are, if not moral philosophers, moral historians, and that's better" (6:92). This distinction between moral philosophers and moral historians, a distinction that relates to the difference between an "experimental" and "dogmatical" approach, also points to the principal experience elicited by strong essay writing: Experience is "moral," though not in the didactic sense of leading the reader to a particular positive or negative position. As in his discussion of Shakespeare's play *Measure for Measure,* Hazlitt rejects the common understanding of morality as being "made up of antipathies" (4:346); rather like Shakespeare, the strong essayist is one who shows "the greatest knowledge of humanity with the greatest fellow-feeling for it" (4:347). Using Montaigne as his model, Hazlitt enumerates how such knowledge can produce a sense of fellow-feeling. Montaigne, first of all, "had the power of looking at things for himself"—that is, he used and revealed himself as a specific example of general humanity. Rejecting the abstract roles of a "philosopher, wit, orator, or moralist," Montaigne dared "to tell us whatever passed through his mind, in its naked simplicity and force" (6:92). One should not be misled by the phrase "whatever passed through his mind." Hazlitt is not advocating indiscriminate impressionism; since Montaigne's was an interesting mind, what passed through it was worth attending to. Obviously, the great danger of the personal essay is that it can easily be written by trivial minds who have limited fellow-feeling and little to reveal about humanity. But, in Hazlitt's eyes, Montaigne is the Shakespeare of the personal essay; his essays are exemplary for their "inexpressible frankness and sincerity, as well as power" (6:93).

Now the question is, how do we distinguish the personal essay from the egotism that Hazlitt repudiates? When, to use Hazlitt's words, do we know that a writer truly has "the courage to say as an author what he felt as a man"? The answer to both questions is expressed in Hazlitt's simple and surprising observation in "Common Places" (#40) that "The object of books is to teach us ignorance; that is to throw a veil over nature" (20:126). This is a remarkable—and seemingly contradictory—comment for an author of books to make; it amounts to saying the best books are those that are not books. What Hazlitt is getting at is that too many authors are enamored of themselves and their reputations as "authors" of books. They "throw a veil over nature" by not revealing themselves as men so much as they advertise themselves as celebrities. Here again Montaigne serves as Hazlitt's model, for Montaigne is a writer who does not address himself to his reader as an "author of books." Hazlitt asserts that Montaigne "did not, in the abstract character of an author, undertake to say all that could be said upon a subject, but what in his capacity as an inquirer after truth he happened to know about it" (6:92). Hazlitt then praises Montaigne, paradoxically, as "the first author who was not a bookmaker. . . . We know not which to be most charmed with, the author or the man" (6:93).[3]

One mark, therefore, of strong essay writing is the purposeful blurring of the distinction between author and man. The attributes of courage, frankness, sincerity, and power are all interrelated in the personal essay: They arise from a strong moral desire to reveal the many facets of humanity and to elicit a sense of fellow-feeling between author and reader, as individuals and representatives of mankind. If, as Hazlitt argues in his essay "On Pedantry," the "perfection of letters is when the highest ambition of the writer is to please his readers, and the greatest pride of the reader is to understand his author" (4:83), that shared pleasure and understanding can only occur, in Hazlitt's view, when writers speak as men, not authors.

Much of Hazlitt's commitment to this position, and to Montaigne's essay in particular, stems from his rejection of the powerful authorial presence of Samuel Johnson. For Hazlitt, Johnson was the most conspicuous example of a writer who spoke as a "bookmaker" and whose method tended to be more dogmatic than experimental. Before we proceed any further, it is important to understand that Hazlitt's differences with Johnson are largely a matter of taste and preference; like Hazlitt, Johnson chose his own models, developed his own voice, and produced his own vision of humanity. In short, Johnson requires no defense. But Hazlitt's response to Johnson is just as revealing from a negative standpoint as his praise of Montaigne is from a positive one. To examine Hazlitt's criticism of Johnson is to understand Hazlitt's defense and praise of personal authorship.

The Example of Samuel Johnson

In "On the Periodical Essayists," Hazlitt suggests that Johnson's alleged faults as a writer include the following: a lack of "relaxation and variety of manner" (6:101); a style that "reduces all things to the same artificial and unmeaning level" (6:102); the mechanical vision of "a complete balance-master in the topics of morality. . . . [He] never encourages hope, but he counteracts it by fear . . . never elicits a truth, but he suggests some objection in answer to it" (6:102); and a "general indisposition to sympathise heartily and spontaneously with works of high-wrought passion or imagination" (6:30). Although Hazlitt has enormous respect for Johnson as a learned author devoted to the art and craft of writing, he nevertheless disputes the *way* Johnson writes—a way that, in Hazlitt's view, is calculated to sustain the distinction between author and man and thereby weaken the tradition of personal authorship.

Briefly stated, Hazlitt argues that Johnson represents the "artificial" style—the opposite of Montaigne's sincerity, frankness, and power. Contending that Johnson's style is basically written "in one key" (7:310), Hazlitt enumerates the main features of this "artificial" style: "It selects a certain set of words to represent all ideas whatever, as the most dignified and elegant, and excludes all others as low and vulgar. The words are not fitted to the things, but the things to the words. Every thing is seen through a false medium. It is putting a mask on the face of nature . . . and completely destroys all force, expression, truth and character, by arbitrarily confounding the differences of things, and reducing everything to the same insipid standard" (7:310–11).

This passage assumes a number of key distinctions: that between low and high style, an organic style (fitting words to things) as distinguished from an artificial style (fitting things to words), variety versus uniformity, and the art of writing as simply mastery of technique as distinguished from the art of writing as personal expression. These distinctions flow from Hazlitt's general preoccupation with the idea that authors of essays can either write as "men" or as "authors." That is, like Montaigne, they can reveal nature personally, or, like Johnson, they can put "a mask on the face of nature." The "mask" Hazlitt refers to is the mask of "authorship"; this is a "false medium" because it places too great an emphasis on the conscious manipulation of language, on the importance of pattern rather than spontaneity, and on the value of intellect rather than personal experience. Thus Hazlitt crisply observes that although Johnson's "subjects are familiar"—that is, they involve the common experiences so important to the fellow-feeling of the personal essay—Johnson nevertheless addresses his readers as an "author [who] is always upon stilts" (6:101).

As much as Hazlitt criticizes and combats the "stilts" of authorship, he quite consistently and revealingly feels nothing but warmth and admiration for the man Samuel Johnson. He genuinely laments that the voice of the man, as recorded in James Boswell's *Life of Samuel*

Johnson, rarely emerges in Johnson's essays. In praising the man in Boswell's *Life,* Hazlitt provides us with a summary of what he expects from himself as well as other authors of the personal essay: "The most triumphant record of the talents and character of Johnson is to be found in Boswell's Life of him. The man was superior to the author. When he threw aside his pen . . . he became not only learned and thoughtful, but acute, witty, humourous, natural, honest. . . . The life and dramatic play of his conversations forms a contrast to his written works. His natural powers and undisguised opinions were called out in convivial intercourse. . . . Johnson's colloquial style was as blunt, direct, and downright, as his style of studied composition was involved and circuitous" (6:102–103).

Where Johnson—in Hazlitt's eyes—failed as an author, but not as a man, was in his inability or unwillingness to adopt a style equal to the goals of personal authorship. As Ian Jack observed, "the essayist limits himself to illustrating the workings of the human mind as they have fallen under his own observation."[4] Samuel Johnson's essays certainly display a profound interest in the workings of the human mind, but where they fall short, according to Hazlitt, is in their substitution of general philosophical observations for specific personal experiences. Put another way, Hazlitt rejects Johnson's abstract authorial style, but commends his personal conversational style. The difference between these two styles lies at the heart of Hazlitt's conception of the personal essay and has been accurately distinguished by Albrecht: "Despite [Hazlitt's] frequent use of parallelism, . . . the structure of Hazlitt's sentences, paragraphs, and essays usually suggests organic growth rather than formal planning—the spontaneous flow of association rather than the exact calculations of reason to which Hazlitt objected so strenuously in Dr. Johnson's style. . . . The progress in Hazlitt's familiar essays is almost always spiral."[5]

Hazlitt's Conversational Style

Why was Johnson the man, superior to Johnson the author? The answer is clearly because, as seen by Hazlitt, his conversation revealed his "natural powers and undisguised opinions." It is not just what Johnson said in conversation, but how he said it—in other words, the personal voice that emerged. Where Johnson's "style of studied composition was involved and circuitous," his personal conversational voice was "blunt, direct, and downright"—the very characteristics of Hazlitt's personal voice. For example, in his preface to *A View of the English Stage,* Hazlitt declares about his own writing voice: "My opinions have been sometimes called singular; they are merely sincere. I say what I think; I think what I feel. I cannot help receiving certain impressions from things; and I have sufficient courage [echoing his view of Montaigne] to declare (somewhat abruptly) what they are" (5:175).

The distinction between a literary and conversational style is an obsession with Hazlitt, chiefly because he wishes to align the focus of literature with personal experience. To avoid writing on "stilts," Hazlitt cultivates a personal voice based on a conversational model, the model of informed people conversing as they sit around a table. *Table-Talk* is a remarkably wide-ranging collection of essays that touches on such topics as painting (including Sir Joshua Reynolds's *Discourses on Art*), different kinds of writing style, mental qualities, literary criticism, politics, the fear of death; and there is even a caustic essay on will making, in which Hazlitt wryly comments that "The art of will-making chiefly consists in baffling the importunity of expectation" (8:117).

In the advertisement to the Paris edition of *Table-Talk* (1821), Hazlitt describes the style and overall purpose of his essays:

The title may perhaps serve to explain what there is of peculiarity in the style or mode of treating the subjects. I had remarked that when I had written or thought upon a particular topic, and afterwards had occasion to speak of it with a friend, the conversation generally took a much wider range, and branched off into a number of indirect and collateral questions, which were not strictly connected with the original view of the subject, but which often threw a curious and striking light upon it, or human life in general. It therefore occurred to me as possible to combine the advantages of these two styles, the *literary* and *conversational*; or after stating and enforcing some leading idea, to follow it up by such observations and reflections as would probably suggest themselves in discussing the same question in company with others. This seemed to me to promise a greater variety and richness, and perhaps a greater sincerity, than could be attained by a more precise and scholastic method. (8:333)

Hazlitt's desire to blend the two modes of a literary and conversational style frequently leads him to meditate on his own ability (or inability) to create an authentic writing voice. Two essays in *Table-Talk* express his preoccupation with creating a writing voice convincingly adapted to the familiar essay.[6] The first essay, entitled "Character of

Cobbett," quite appropriately focuses on Hazlitt's contemporary, William Cobbett, who was famous for his blunt and outspoken essays. As much as Hazlitt and Cobbett differed on specific issues, Hazlitt's admiration—and possibly emulation—of his style is evident throughout. Describing Cobbett as not only "the most powerful political writer of the present day, but one of the best writers in the language" (8:50), Hazlitt details those characteristics that make an effective conversational style.

To begin with, Hazlitt observes that Cobbett "speaks and thinks plain, broad downright English" (8:50). In praising Cobbett's style, Hazlitt is also describing his own ideals as an author.[7] Furthermore, Cobbett passes Hazlitt's test of originality that "a really great and original writer is like nobody but himself" (8:50). That is, Cobbett's uniqueness and power are, paradoxically, indescribable. We have seen before how much Hazlitt defends the tacit nature of the imagination; and here again—as in his examinations of Burke, Shakespeare, and Montaigne—Hazlitt uses the author's originality as a demonstration of the proposition that "It is easy to describe second-rate talents, because they fall into a class, and enlist under a standard: but first-rate powers defy calculation or comparison, and can be defined only by themselves" (8:51). Moreover, just as Hazlitt defends Montaigne's form of egotism, so he differentiates between Cobbett's egotism—a basic ingredient of personal authorship—and the affectation of second-rate writers. Hazlitt argues that Cobbett "does not talk of himself for lack of something to write about, but because some circumstance that has happened to himself is the best possible illustration of the subject. . . . His egotism is full of individuality, and has room for very little vanity in it" (8:52–53).

How strongly Hazlitt prizes such individuality can be seen in the essay "The Indian Jugglers" (1819), which may well be Hazlitt's finest personal expression of how original creation differs from mechanical excellence. If first-rate writers are, as Hazlitt says, "*sui generis,* and make the class to which they belong" (8:51), why can't the same be said of the perfection of mechanical excellence, as with jugglers? The answer is the same one provided in "Why the Arts Are Not Progressive," but the manner of the answer, quite appropriately, is more personal.

Watching the Indian jugglers juggle four balls at the same time Hazlitt wonders, "Is it then a trifling power we see at work, or is it not something next to miraculous?" (8:77). That is, can it not be said that the jugglers have achieved the originality of art—an originality that Hazlitt, at least initially, finds personally humbling, if not downright humiliating? Hazlitt writes:

> I ask what there is that I can do as well as this? Nothing. What have I been doing all my life? Have I been idle, or have I nothing to show for all my labour and pains? . . . Is there no one thing in which I can challenge competition, that I can bring as an instance of exact perfection, in which others cannot find a flaw? The utmost I can pretend to do is to write a description of what this fellow can do. I can write a book; so can many others who have not even learned to spell. . . . Instead of writing on four subjects at a time, it is as much as I can manage to keep the thread of one discourse clear and untangled. (8:79)

Lest we dismiss such writing as mere self-indulgence, Hazlitt extracts an important observation from his personal experience: His awareness of the juggler's excellence, as compared with his own labor as a writer, elicits "this feeling of the inefficacy and slow progress of intellectual compared to mechanical excellence, and it has always made me somewhat dissatisfied" (8:79). Hazlitt's sense of dissatisfaction is pertinent, for, though the goal of writing may theoretically be perfection, it is finally an unattainable goal. Unlike in writing, "perfection in mechanical exercises is the performing certain feats to a uniform nicety, that is, in fact, undertaking no more than you can perform" (8:81). A juggler may practice to perfection, but every time a writer composes he faces new challenges and obstacles. Unlike balls, words and sentences do not follow the physical laws of nature. A writer necessarily and continually faces the unexpected, for his goal is to imitate and reveal nature: What perfection there is will be nature's, not the writer's. Thus the central point of "The Indian Jugglers" is to distinguish between the power and purpose of writing as a creative act and the power and purpose of juggling as a mechanical art. For Hazlitt, the power behind writing is "indifferently called genius, imagination, feeling, taste; but the manner in which it acts upon the mind can neither be defined by abstract rules, as is the case in science, nor verified by continual unvarying experiments, as is the case in mechanical performances" (8:83).

Having asserted both the need for uniqueness in the essay on Cobbett and the general nature of such uniqueness in "The Indian Jugglers," Hazlitt is naturally led to wonder how the imagination through the personal essay "acts upon the mind" of readers. Here Hazlitt stakes his claim on the very uneven grounds of common sense—uneven because common sense is difficult terrain to define.[8] Nevertheless, to understand how Hazlitt develops his conversational style and expands the range of the familiar essay, we need to examine his basic distinction between "common sense" and "commonplace."

Common Sense versus Commonplace

In his essay "Common Sense" (1829), Hazlitt asserts that "Common sense and *common place* are also the antipodes of each other: the one is a collection of true experiences, the other a routine of cant phrases. All affectation is the death of common sense, which requires the utmost simplicity and sincerity" (20:291–92). We already know that the personal style of simplicity and sincerity, as distinguished from the artificial style of writing upon "stilts," is a model Hazlitt takes from Montaigne; but it is reasonable to ask what constitutes the "true experiences" of common sense. Here, several of Hazlitt's essays from *Table-Talk* are helpful—in particular, "On Genius and Common Sense," "On the Ignorance of the Learned," and "On Familiar Style."

Focusing on the latter essay first, we see that Hazlitt again distinguishes between the familiar style and the high style of Samuel Johnson that is described as having "no discrimination, no selection, no variety in it" (8:243). "To write a genuine familiar or truly English style," Hazlitt says, "is to write as any one would speak in common conversaion, who had a thorough command and choice of words, or who could discourse with ease, force, and perspecuity, setting aside all pedantic and oratorical flourishes" (8:242). Such a style, Hazlitt argues, "can never be quaint or vulgar, for this reason, that it is of universal force and applicability" (8:243). That is, the focus of the style is on specific but common human experiences, experiences that are "true" in the sense that they are shared: They form a bond of familiarity between writer and reader.

If, as Hazlitt observes, the "proper force of words lies not in the words themselves, but in their application" (8:244), that application in the personal essay must tap the writer's and reader's "common sense." A familiar style, like the familiar essay, is based on the awareness that "common sense is only a judge of things that fall under common observation, or immediately come home to the business and bosoms of men. This is of the very essence of its principle, the basis of its pretensions. It rests upon the simple process of feeling, it anchors in experience. It is not, nor cannot be, the test of abstract, speculative opinions" (8:37). We have seen in previous chapters how committed Hazlitt is to "feeling," and how limiting he believes "abstract, speculative opinions" to be. Because Hazlitt feels so strongly about the tacit understanding that guides human behavior, he naturally enough sees the personal essay as a vehicle for expressing "common sense," which is another term for tacit knowledge. Hazlitt is by no means rejecting intellectual truths, but he is clearly removing such intellectual interests from the scope of the personal essay. If, as Hazlitt says, "common sense is only a judge of things that fall under common observation," then it surely follows that the personal essay, whose main focus is on "common sense," is the most appropriate literary vehicle for expressing "common observations," as distinguished from abstract opinions.

Earlier in this chapter we heard Hazlitt say, "the object of books is to teach us ignorance; that is, to throw a veil over nature" (20:126). Once again, in *Table-Talk,* he returns to this observation as a way of defining the purpose of the personal essay. This time he entitles an essay "On the Ignorance of the Learned," and he deals not just with learned authors, but also with learned readers. Hazlitt's reasoning is simply stated, though not simpleminded: In his view, "Learning is, in too many cases, but a foil of common sense; a substitute for true knowledge" (8:70). He then explains in precise detail how learning can become an obstacle and rival to common sense:

Books are less often made use of as 'spectacles' to look at nature with, than as blinds to keep out its strong light and shifting scenery from weak eyes and indolent minds. The book-worm wraps himself up in his web of verbal generalities, and sees only the glimmering shadows of things reflected from the minds of others. Nature *puts him out.* . . . He can only breathe a learned atmosphere, as other men breathe common air. He is a borrower of sense. He has no ideas of his own, and must live on those of other people. . . . The knowledge of that which is before us, or about us, which appeals to our experience, passions, and pursuits, to the bosoms and business of men, is not learning. Learning is the knowledge of that which none but the learned know. He is the most learned man who knows the most of what is farthest removed from common life and actual observation, that is of the least practical utility, and least liable to be brought to the test of experience. (8:70–71, 73)

The key term here is "the test of experience." There are two kinds of knowledge—the abstract and learned, as distinguished from the common and practical. Both have as their focus "nature," but each approaches nature from a vastly different viewpoint. Thus each employs books (or essays) in distinct ways. To use Hazlitt's analogy, learned books—of which Hazlitt himself was an author—tend to operate as "blinds" that shut out nature. Such books are confining in the sense that they are close-ended (or close-minded). Because they are rigidly confined to a thesis, they produce "ignorance" in the paradoxical sense that they substitute abstractions for experience. On the other hand, less learned books—by which Hazlitt really means familiar essays—are designed to open, rather than shut out, vistas of human nature. Instead of seeking abstract knowledge, such personal works appeal to "the bosoms and business of men" by attending to the "knowledge of that which is before us, or about us, which appeals to our experience, passions, and pursuits." Such variety and openness, as we shall now see, are the hallmarks of Hazlitt's best essays.

The Familiar Essay: *The Round Table* and *Table-Talk*

Of the two collections of essays, *The Round Table* (1817) and *Table-Talk* (1821–22), John Kinnaird has commented that the former essays "are 'familiar' enough in the sense of being casually informal" but they "are never intimately personal in the manner of *Table-Talk*."[9] This difference is partly accounted for once we recognize that the literary intent of *The Round Table* is basically imitative. In Hazlitt's words, the essays are written "in the manner of the early periodical Essayists, the Spectator and Tatler" (4:Advertisement). *The Round Table* contains fifty-two essays, twelve of which were written by Leigh Hunt. The focus of the collection, as its original subtitle indicates, is on literature, men, and manners. For the most part, the essays deal more with literary observations than with personal experiences. Only intermittently do the essays in *The Round Table* reveal Hazlitt's mature personal voice and convey his complex understanding of human nature. Three essays, in particular, herald the stronger personal tone of *Table-Talk:* "On the Love of Life," "On Good Nature," and "On Common-Place Critics."

"On Common-Place Critics" is a typical kind of essay written by numerous eighteenth-century periodical essayists. Because literary criticism, of a sort, had become almost an industry during the eighteenth century, analysts of literature tended to repeat, if not mimic, one another's observations. Whatever was fashionable tended to be praised, and whatever was different was frequently condemned. In this essay, Hazlitt intends to accomplish, however briefly, two objectives: to expose and ridicule cant criticism, and, through his own prose style, to demonstrate the real freedom and frankness that can occur by using a more personal voice. In a way, then, Hazlitt is specifically talking about commonplace criticism, but he is also generally discussing commonplace thinking. Hazlitt writes that "A common-place critic has something to say upon every occasion, and he always tells you either what is not true, or what you knew before, or what is not worth knowing. He is a person who thinks by proxy, and talks by rote. He differs with you, not because he thinks you are in the wrong, but because he thinks somebody else will think so" (4:136–37). A commonplace critic (for which we may substitute writer) is thus one who always has an opinion that is 1) not his own, 2) usually misleading, 3) a cliché, or 4) irrelevant. The principal goal of a commonplace critic is to maintain the status quo, for such a writer is more concerned and comfortable with what others think as a group.

Now, for Hazlitt, criticism, like writing generally, must be a liberating activity—an act wherein a writer has the "courage to say as an author what he feels as a man." In effect, commonplace criticism amounts to cowardly writing. What Hazlitt repudiates is a "person who thinks by proxy, and talks by rote"—a writer who echoes the opinions and judgments of others. When Hazlitt labels a commonplace critic as a "pedant of polite conversation" (4:139), he means the objective of such a writer is simply to reinforce the prevailing platitudes of a select audience who imagine themselves the best company and people of "good sense." Adopting one of his favorite stylistic maneuvers, Hazlitt resorts to an epigrammatic characterization of commonplace standards. He describes "good sense" as the "opinions of a number of persons who have agreed to take their opinions on trust from others"; he calls the "select forms" of commonplace "the accredited language of conventional impertinence," and he memorably sums up the "best company" as "persons who live on their own estates, and other people's ideas" (4:137). It is no wonder that Hazlitt's best essay writing has been described as conveying "a strong forensic thrust that spurns equivocation."[10] Hazlitt views such equivocation and servility as representative of commonplace thinking and writing.

The reverse of commonplace writing is seen in Hazlitt's two essays, "On the Love of Life" and "On Good Nature." In these essays his personal voice and unconventional views emerge powerfully and purpose-fully. Always one to adopt a surprising slant, Hazlitt turns the commonplace into uncommon sense. For example, in "On the Love of Life" he expresses his general desire to "expose certain vulgar errors, which have crept into our reasoning on men and manners" (4:1). He then states, in a rather startling way, his specific interest: "Our notions with respect to the importance of life, and our attachment to it, depend on a principle, which has very little to do with its happiness or misery" (4:1). Do we love life (if indeed we do love life) because we enjoy it? No, says Hazlitt; happiness has nothing to do with our attachment to life. Rather, "The love of life is, in general, the effect not of our en-joyments, but of our passions" (4:1).

Passion is the key principle that explains our determined hold on life; in this instance, the passion is our fear of death. Arguing that the "strength of the passion seldom corresponds to the pleasure we find in its indulgence" (4:3), Hazlitt focuses, in highly personal terms, on how our love of life is determined by our fear of death: "However weary we may be of the same stale round—however sick of the past—however hopeless of the future—the mind still revolts at the thought of death, because the fancied possibility of good, which always remains with life, gathers strength as it is about to be torn from us for ever, and the dullest scene looks bright compared with the darkness of the grave" (4:2). Thus, the phrase "the love of life" has less to do with the affir-mation of life than the fear of death. We are firmly attached to life, even more so in the midst of the greatest misery, because our passions daily tell us that "To be something [namely, alive] is better than to be nothing [that is, dead]" (4:3).

Just as Hazlitt cunningly dissects the commonplace about "the love of life," so he even more effectively exposes another commonplace in "On Good Nature." Thought to be a virtue, good nature, according to Hazlitt, "is the most selfish of all the virtues: It is nine times out of ten mere indolence of disposition" (4:100–101). An alert reader quickly wonders what Hazlitt means by "selfish virtue." We have not long to wait to see that "good nature," in Hazlitt's view, combines self-interest with a passive response to the needs of others. In the most uncompromising manner, Hazlitt argues that a good-natured man "feels no emotions of anger or detestation, if you tell him of the dev-astation of a province, or the massacre of the inhabitants of a town, or the enslaving of a people; but if his dinner is spoiled by a lump of soot falling down the chimney, he is thrown into the utmost confusion, and can hardly recover a decent command of his temper for the whole day" (4:101). A good-natured man is viewed as an egotist on two counts: He is preoccupied with his own pleasure and indifferent to the needs of others. In the same way and for the same reasons, Hazlitt later describes a "well-meaning man" as "one who often does a great deal of mischief without any kind of malice" (4:104). Like a good-natured man, a well-meaning man is only so at his convenience; neither man makes an effort that could possibly involve some form of inconvenience or self-sacrifice. Rather, they are only active, paradoxically, in defense of their own passive self-interested way of life.

How deeply Hazlitt feels about such passive virtues is seen in his hostile observation that "Good-nature is humanity that costs nothing. No good-natured man was ever a martyr to a cause, in religion or politics" (4:102). Hazlitt thus turns the ostensible subject of his essay—good nature—into a defense of its apparent opposite: so-called "badnatured" people. That is, if good nature is "humanity that costs nothing," then Hazlitt figures that bad nature—at least in his case— is humanity willing to give a lot, sometimes at great cost. Clearly thinking of himself, as well as many other reformers who possess a sharp sense of injustice, Hazlitt asserts:

If the truth were known, the most disagreeable people are the most amiable. They are the only persons who feel an interest in what does not concern them. They have as much regard for others as they have for themselves. They have as many vexations and causes of complaint as there are in the world. They are genuine righters of wrongs, and redresser of grievances. . . . They have an unfortunate attachment to a set of abstract phrases, such as *liberty, truth, justice, humanity, honour,* which are continually abused by knaves, and misunderstood by fools, and they can hardly contain themselves for spleen. (4:101–102)

Why are the most disagreeable people amiable? The answer is, because they care about the well-being of others, particularly those who cannot defend themselves. Indeed, the disagreeableness of disagreeable people is a measure of their concern for humanity, just as the good nature of good-natured people is an index of their indifference for others. If disagreeable people, as Hazlitt says, are in perpetual hot water, good-natured people pour cold water on real emotion. Never one to shun a paradox, Hazlitt suggests that "The definition of a true patriot is a *good hater*" (4:103); his love for people leads him to hate human indifference and social injustice.

The hostile tone of "On Good Nature" is not generally representative of the essays in *The Round Table* and *Table-Talk*. It is, however, representative of Hazlitt's *Political Essays,* to which we shall now turn.

Hazlitt's Political "Characters"

No examination of Hazlitt's essays would be complete without a look at his use of "character" writing. This type of writing has a long history that is well suited to Hazlitt's moral and political views. Indeed, as we shall see, no form of writing more agreed with Hazlitt's talent and temperament. Hazlitt is at his controversial best when he writes "characters."

Traditionally, the purpose of character writing was "to describe a type or class of mankind, not an individual person."[11] Thus there are many traditional characters written on such general topics as the virtuous man, the avaricious man, the prudent man, etc. But this is not how Hazlitt uses the tradition. Speaking of *The Spirit of the Age,* Ian Jack comments: "What Hazlitt had done is to invent a new kind of 'character' writing. Drawing on his knowledge of the 'characters' which may be found in the literature of the seventeenth and eighteenth centuries he has evolved a new species of literary character in which the subject is neither the author as an individual nor his writings regarded in themselves, but the author as an author, in his works, and as a representative of the *Zeitgeist.*"[12]

What Jack is suggesting is that Hazlitt developed a way of accommodating character writing to the familiar essay; and he did so by ignoring the traditional interest in a type or class of mankind, and instead by focusing on real historical individuals as representative of a general type. To put it bluntly, Hazlitt adapted the literary character to the familiar essay in such a way that familiarity was made to breed contempt. Hazlitt's characters tend to be his most powerful expression of moral outrage.[13]

Political Essays was published in 1819. It was designed as, in Hazlitt's words, "Sketches of Public Characters," complete with an epigraph announcing Hazlitt's intent: "Come, draw the curtain, shew the picture." By and large, the picture Hazlitt shows highlights a sense of disgust and moral outrage. As he declares in the preface to this volume, "I am no politician, and still less can I be said to be a party-man; but I have a hatred of tyranny, and a contempt for its tools; and this feeling I have expressed as often and as strongly as I could" (7:7). Within this fifteen-page preface, Hazlitt provides the reader with a number of minicharacters that at once demonstrate the conciseness of his character writing, the strength of his moral convictions, and his general contempt for politics and politicians. Of political reformers, Hazlitt writes: "A Reformer never is—but always to be blest, in the accomplishment of his airy hopes and shifting schemes of progressive perfectibility. . . . He would rather have slavery than liberty, unless it is liberty precisely after his own fashion" (7:15). On the other hand, the Tory—the political opposite of a Reformer—is not any better. Of the character of a Tory, Hazlitt observes: "His principle is to follow the leader; and this is the infallible rule to have numbers and success on your side. . . . Power is the rock of his salvation" (7:17). With the Reformers and Tories brushed aside, Hazlitt then turns to the Whigs as the apparent compromisers, but they, too, are rejected: "A Whig is properly what is called a Trimmer—that is, a coward to both sides of a question, who dares not be a knave nor an honest man, but is a sort of whiffling, shuffling, cunning, silly, contemptible, unmeaning negation of the two" (7:21).

Why, one might reasonably ask, does Hazlitt express so much hostility in such characters? The answer has to do with his lifelong fear of what abstractions and institutions can do to people. Most of all he fears, though he is not immune to, the delusions of abstractions and the corruption of institutions. This concern is strongly stated in another character essay entitled "On Corporate Bodies." Hazlitt writes: "Corporate bodies are more corrupt and profligate than individuals, because they have more power to do mischief, and are less amenable to disgrace or punishment. They feel neither shame, remorse, gratitude, nor goodwill. The principle of private or natural conscience is extinguished in each individual (we have no moral sense in the breasts of others), and nothing is considered but how the united efforts of the whole (released from idle scruples) may be best directed to the obtaining of political advantages and privileges to be shared as common spoil" (8:264). Hazlitt's fear of institutions—of how they can corrupt individuals—is summed up in a single memorable sentence: "Public bodies are so far worse than individuals composing them, because the *official* takes place of the *moral sense*" (8:265).

Almost all of Hazlitt's characters—favorable or unfavorable—work variations of the distinction and collision between the official and moral sense. In two of his early political characters—"Character of Mr. Pitt" (1806) and "Character of Lord Chatham" (1807)—Hazlitt deals with such a collision of values. Interestingly, the two characters are also portraits of father and son. William Pitt the Younger (1759–1806) was the prime minister of England during the French Revolutionary Wars. He was an enemy of both the French Revolution and of Napoleon. His father, William Pitt the Elder (1708–78), whom Hazlitt addresses as Lord Chatham, was also a prime minister during wartime—the Seven Years' War (1756–63). Known as the "Great Commoner," William Pitt, the Elder (Lord Chatham) is characterized favorably because of his strong advocacy of, among other things, the American colonies.

In the case of Mr. Pitt, Hazlitt represents him as an antirevolutionary who is the consummate politician—all ease and verbal facility, but no moral convictions. Hazlitt characterizes him as a man who achieved a reputation "for the possession of every moral excellence" by a negation of "the common vices of human nature, and by the complete negation of every other talent that might interfere with the only one he possessed in a supreme degree . . . an artful use of words, and a certain dexterity of logical arrangement" (7:322). In Hazlitt's view, Pitt's use of language is calculated to promote an official sense at the expense of moral conviction. As Hazlitt caustically remarks, Pitt "seemed not to have believed that the truth of his statements depended on the reality of the facts, but that the things depended on the order in which he arranged them in words" (7:323–24). Moreover, just as Hazlitt views Pitt's language as empty of substance, so he characterizes Pitt as a man devoid of moral sense. Of his moral deficiency, Hazlitt writes: "having no general principles, no comprehensive views of things, no moral habits of thinking, no system of action, there was nothing to hinder him from pursuing any particular purpose, by any means that offered" (7:322–23).

By contrast, Lord Chatham—Pitt's father—is described as that rare politician whose moral sense remained intact. Unlike his son, Chatham "spoke as a man should speak, because he felt as a man should feel" (7:297). Such praise, of course, echoes Hazlitt's praise of Montaigne. Chatham was a politician who had the courage to speak as a minister— as Montaigne had as a writer—what he felt as a man. Instead of propagandizing, as Pitt is accused of having done, Chatham is praised as a man for whom the "feelings and the rights of Englishmen were enshrined in his heart" (7:297). The highest compliment Hazlitt can pay to Chatham, or any other person is that "The whole man moved under this impulse. He felt the cause of liberty as his own" (7:297). To think morally is to feel the cause of liberty: This is the message of the American and French revolutions. This identification of morality and liberty, in opposition to any form of "official" sense, may help us explain Hazlitt's controversial adulation of Napoleon.

To put it directly and doubtless controversially, Hazlitt views Napoleon as a libertarian who opposed the most dreaded form of an "official" sense: legitimacy. One may question Hazlitt's historical judgment, but there is no doubting his sincerity and consistency.[14] Hazlitt's *Life of Napoleon Buonaparte* (1828–30) was his final major work, and it was clearly designed to summarize and celebrate the man whose character best expressed Hazlitt's political views. As Hazlitt writes in the preface to *The Life of Napoleon Buonaparte:*

> what chiefly attached me to him, was his being . . . 'the child and champion of the Revolution.' Of this character he could not divest himself, even though he wished it. He was nothing, he could be nothing but what he owed to himself and to his triumphs over those who claimed mankind as their inheritance by a divine right; and as long as he was *a thorn in the side of kings* and kept them at bay, his cause rose out of the ruins and defeat of their pride and hopes of revenge. . . . This was the chief point at issue . . . Whether mankind were, from the beginning to the end of time, born slaves or not? As long as he remained, his acts, his very existence gave a proud and full answer to this question. (13:ix)

Regarding himself as a child and champion of the French Revolution, Hazlitt identifies with Napoleon as a thorn in the side of kings and their supporting doctrine of legitimacy. Indeed, in the preface to his *Political Essays* Hazlitt condemns the "dungeon" and "plague" of legitimacy and explains how he has escaped being tainted: "I am not leprous all over, the lie of Legitimacy does not fix its mortal sting in my inmost soul, nor, like an ugly spider, entangle me in its slimy folds; but is kept off from me, and broods on its own poison. He who did this for me, and for the rest of the world, and who alone could do it, was Buonaparte" (7:10).

If, as Hazlitt declares, the "motto of legitimacy . . . is in a word inveterate prejudice without reflection and power borrowed from accident," Bonaparte is "the very counterpart and antidote to it, intellect without prejudice and inherent power and greatness" (14:155). In

Hazlitt's eyes, George III broke the peace .of Amiens with Napoleon because the power of legitimacy could not tolerate the character of a leader "who had risen from the people, and who had no power over them but from the services he had rendered them" (14:200). Clearly, Hazlitt sees in Napoleon the greatest character of a liberator, one whose actions embody the most basic values of political and intellectual freedom. In his own distinctive way, Napoleon had the courage as a leader to express what he felt as a man.

Chapter Seven
The Dramatic Imagination

John Kinnaird has suggested that "The fundamental continuity of English criticism from Dryden through Pope, Addison and Johnson to Hazlitt may be said to consist in the simple fact that these critics were all essayists."[1] So far as he goes, Kinnaird is right—but not completely. All these writers were not only essayists, but also, more importantly, they were moral essayists. Where Hazlitt, however, differed from Dryden, Pope, Addison, and Johnson is that he did not share Johnson's assumption that "he that thinks reasonably must think morally."[2] In clear divergence from this rational tradition, Hazlitt gave much greater value to the dramatic (or sympathetic) imagination as both a literary and moral agent. Unlike his eighteenth-century predecessors, Hazlitt saw the imagination, not reason, as the principal means to a greater end: moral understanding.

For example, in an important (though undated) essay entitled "On Reason and Imagination," Hazlitt asserts that "Men act from passion; and we can only judge of passion by sympathy" (12:47). He goes on to say that passion "is the essence, the chief ingredient in moral truth; and the warmth of passion is sure to kindle the light of the imagination on objects around it" (12:46). What Hazlitt does is credit the imagination with powers that were previously reserved—by the likes of Dryden, Pope, Addison, and Johnson—to reason. Asserting that the "boundary of our sympathy is a circle which enlarges itself according to its propulsion from the centre—the heart" (12:55), Hazlitt argues that the integration of imagination and feeling, or sympathy and the heart, enables us to experience the general in the particular, rather than the reverse as numerous eighteenth-century writers would have it.

This reasoning is why Hazlitt in all his writings was so preoccupied with the role of the imagination, and why he was so contentious with figures like Samuel Johnson and Sir Joshua Reynolds, who tend to limit our literary and aesthetic experience to reason. Because Hazlitt believed that "Moral and poetical truth is like expression in a picture—the one is not to be attained by smearing over a large canvas, nor the other by bestriding a vague topic" (12:55), he continually focused his attention on individual details, judgments, and even writers. The clearest way that Hazlitt could develop his own approach to the powers of the imagination was to contend with—and sometimes misread—major writers of the past and present. While it is accurate to describe Hazlitt as "a worthy successor to Dryden and Johnson," and to regard him as "a man of letters in the comprehensive sense in which Johnson and Coleridge were men of letters,"[3] we must realize that Hazlitt shaped his fundamental views as a critical rival to such figures as Dryden, Coleridge, and, most importantly, Samuel Johnson. To define his identity and to defend his commitment to the dramatic imagination, Hazlitt continually asserted his own controversial independence.

Criticism and Controversy

In one of his last essays appropriately entitled "The Spirit of Controversy" (1830), Hazlitt expressed his central assumption that "When a thing ceases to be a subject of controversy, it ceases to be a subject of interest" (20:309). Controversy stimulated Hazlitt's imagination; he sought it with animation and animus. He loved a good fight, as is evident in his memorable essay "The Fight" (1822) (17:72–86). The fight that Hazlitt describes serves as an analogue to his fondness for controversy and confrontation. We can easily detect how stimulated his imagination becomes as he records the drama of a fight. He writes: "to see two men smashed to the ground, smeared with gore, stunned, senseless, the breath beaten out of their bodies; and then, before you recover from the shock, to see them rise up with new strength and courage, stand steady to inflict or receive mortal offence, and rush upon each other 'like two clouds over the Caspian'—this is the most astonishing thing of all:—this is the high and heroic state of man!" (17:82).

Clearly, Hazlitt fancied himself a fighter, if not a hero. Although John Mahoney is correct to emphasize about Hazlitt that "almost from the beginning there is the sense in his life and writing that he is in the minority,"[4] it is necessary to recall that, however much he was in the minority, he could rarely be accused, as Hazlitt said of John Horne Tooke, that he "represented nobody but himself" (11:51). Hazlitt's combativeness excited his imagination and provided moral force to his writing; but the writing itself was focused on what he took to be the expression of basic human needs.

In another late essay "A Farewell to Essay-Writing" (1828), Hazlitt reflects on his life and observes: "What sometimes surprises me in looking back to the past, is . . . to find myself so little changed in the time. The same images and trains of thought stick by me: I have the same tastes, likings, sentiments, and wishes that I had then" (17:316). Many of those images and trains of thought originated with his early desire to "chastise the presumption of modern philosophy," whose advocates he asserts, "by an exclusive and constant claim to the privilege of reason, have so completely satisfied themselves, and so very nearly persuaded others to believe that they are the only rational persons in the world" (*Letters,* 15 February 1809:106). But if Hazlitt is suspicious of an overemphasis on reason, he is no less critical and controversial in his remarks about an egotistical preoccupation with the imagination. For Hazlitt, as Albrecht has observed, "imagination and feeling became increasingly recognized as allies against selfishness."[5] As we have seen in *The Spirit of the Age,* Hazlitt's attacks on many of the romantic poets are unrelenting. He severely criticizes romanticism on the grounds that many of its poets—Wordsworth, Coleridge, Byron, Shelley—often marched to the tune of an egotistic conception of the imagination, at the same time that some of them (Wordsworth, Coleridge, Southey, Scott) lined up behind the political banner of Legitimacy.

We may also see Hazlitt's controversial independence in the way he reads (and misreads) Edmund Burke. As we have seen, he regards Burke as a political antagonist and dreaded enemy of the French Revolution; in this regard, Burke is seen as a spokesman for Legitimacy. But Hazlitt also uses Burke to identify his own view of what constitutes genius, imagination, and originality; he draws from Burke's example the need to assert one's views, however controversial, with power and purpose. Throughout his career, Burke expresses what Hazlitt calls "untameable vigour and originality" (7:310), the very attributes that Hazlitt himself sought in his own writings. But where Hazlitt lauds Burke's imagination as one that "never became set . . . [that] was in further search and progress,"—as, in short, an imagination that was continually creative—he no less forcefully rejects Burke's friend and contemporary, Samuel Johnson, as a writer who, unwittingly or not, stifled the imagination because he so strongly distrusted it. In his opposition to Samuel Johnson, Hazlitt summarizes his own distinctive views of the dramatic imagination.

Hazlitt's Opposition to Johnson's Criticism

Although not a great deal has previously been said about it, there is no way to overestimate Johnson's influence on Hazlitt. Even a casual survey of the general index to Hazlitt's collected works clearly reveals that Johnson was constantly in Hazlitt's mind. For an aspiring literary critic, Johnson was unquestionably the frame of reference; he was the man whose views of literature must be reckoned with. Anxious to establish himself as a literary critic, Hazlitt understandably felt intimidated by the presence and performance of Johnson. To define himself he needed to dispute with Johnson.

Hazlitt's central objection, as he states it in his review of Farington's *Life of Sir Joshua Reynolds* (1820), was to Johnson's rational habit of referring "every thing to distinct principles and a visible origin" (16:186). This is a habit that obscures, if not suppresses, the fundamentally tacit nature of works of genius, whose chief attributes Hazlitt describes as "ease, simplicity, and freedom from conscious effort" (16:188). Hazlitt is so firmly committed to the position that genius and imagination are tacit powers—powers whose origin and effects are not susceptible of intellectual formulations—that, in a characteristically unconventional estimate, he asserts the superiority of Oliver Goldsmith's imagination over Johnson's. Comparing Johnson's periodical, *The Rambler,* with Goldsmith's periodical, *The Citizen of the World,* Hazlitt declares Goldsmith to be "more observing, more original, more natural and picturesque than Johnson" (6:104). Hazlitt willingly concedes the strength of Johnson's intellect, at the same time that he condemns the limitations of his imagination. As a critic, Johnson explicitly formulates positions and problems, but precisely because his intellect is so powerful he either withdraws from or is unresponsive to the "affective openness"[6] of a literary imagination like Goldsmith's.

Even in his understanding of the novel, Hazlitt parts company with the prevailing Johnsonian view. In his lecture "On the English Novelists" (1819), Hazlitt responds to Johnson's assertion of the superiority of Samuel Richardson's fiction over Henry Fielding's by observing: "Dr. Johnson seems to have preferred this truth of reflection to the truth of nature, when he said that there was more knowledge of the human heart in a page of Richardson, than in all Fielding" (6:119). As Hazlitt sees it, the issue does not involve knowledge per se, but rather what Roy Park has aptly called the "experiential response"[7] to imaginative truths. It amounts to a question of emphasis: Do we read fiction for knowledge, or do we read fiction as a stimulus to our own experience, in which case our response to fiction is much more open-ended? Hazlitt formulates this distinction very precisely in *Characteristics* (#135): "Nature is stronger than reason: for nature is, after all, the text, reason but the comment. He is indeed a poor creature who does not *feel* the truth of more than he *knows* or can explain satisfactorily to others" (9:189).

In reaction to Johnson, Hazlitt explains what he means by "truth of reflection" when he says of Richardson's fiction: "Richardson's nature is always the nature of sentiment and reflection, not of impulse or situation. He furnishes his characters, on every occasion, with the presence of mind of the author. He makes them act, not as they would from the impulse of the moment, but as they might upon reflection. . . . Every thing is too conscious in his works" (6:119). "Consciousness" and "presence of mind" are attributes that Johnson looks for in literature; for Hazlitt, however, such attributes frequently prevent Richardson's characters from stimulating the reader's own imaginative participation in their dramatic predicaments. Because Richardson's "real excellence lies in his representation of the ideal forms of passion and imagination," his novels certainly have a strong mental appeal—something Johnson approves. But this appeal, in Hazlitt's view, limits the reader's response because he believes the power of the dramatic imagination is more forcefully exerted through the representation of concrete experiences.

By contrast, the "truth of nature," as Hazlitt understands it, is less the opposite of the "truth of reflection" in so much as it elicits a more imaginative and comprehensive response to human experience. With disarming candor, Hazlitt cheerfully acknowledges that Fielding's novels are *not* remarkable for "sentiment, nor imagination, nor wit, not even humour"—a statement that seemingly strips Fielding of just about every artistic virtue. What Fielding is remarkable for is "profound knowledge of human nature, at least of English nature" (6:113). Perhaps the key phrase is "English nature," for, in Hazlitt's view, Fielding's *English* understanding, his sense of national character, enables him to individuate rather than idealize his characters. Praising Fielding's "masterly pictures of the characters of men as he saw them existing," Hazlitt continues, "As a painter of real life, he was equal to Hogarth; as a mere observer of human nature, he was little inferior to Shakespeare, though without any of the genius and poetical qualities of his mind. . . . His representations . . . are local and individual; but they are not the less profound and conclusive. The feeling of the general principles of human nature operating in particular circumstances, is always intense, and uppermost in his mind; and he makes use of incident and situation only to bring out character" (6:113).

Clearly the purposes of literature, as understood by Johnson and

Hazlitt, differ widely. Unlike Johnson, Hazlitt assigned a less important role to consciousness, control, and intellect in art; in his view they
tended to produce an art that was imaginatively confining. For Hazlitt,
Johnson's critical approach—which was the preeminent eighteenth-
century approach—depended on a conception of the imagination that
was antithetical to Hazlitt's understanding of imaginative literature.
Where Hazlitt endorsed the tacit appeal of the imagination and asserted the power of feeling as the fullest expression of the imagination,
Johnson, whose "general powers of reasoning overlaid his critical sus-
ceptibility" (4:175), imposed his intellect to counterbalance the vola-
tile power of the imagination. Thus Hazlitt observes, "If he [Johnson]
had the same capacity for following the flights of a truly poetic imagination, or for feeling the finer touches of nature, that he had felicity
and force in detecting and exposing the aberrations from the broad and
beaten path of propriety and common sense, he would have amply
deserved the reputation he has acquired as a philosophical critic"
(6:49).

The Didactic versus the Dramatic Imagination

The crux of the matter here centers on two essentially different views
of how the imagination works and how literature conveys meaning. In
response to Johnson's criticism, Hazlitt establishes a distinction between the didactic and dramatic uses of the imagination. There is no
question that Hazlitt often overstates his case, but in this instance his
distinction highlights and indeed identifies a fundamental change in
literature that occurred between the late eighteenth and early nineteenth centuries. Describing Johnson as a "didactic reasoner," Hazlitt
accurately outlines a way of reading and understanding literature that
he himself does not share. Hazlitt argues in the preface to *Characters of
Shakespear's Plays* that "It is the province of the didactic reasoner to take
cognizance of those results of human nature which are constantly repeated and always the same, which follow one another in regular
succession, which are acted upon by large classes of men, and embodied
in received customs, laws, language, and institutions; and it was in
arranging, comparing, and arguing on these kind of general results
that Johnson's excellence lay" (4:175).

What a didactic reasoner like Johnson seeks, and what a great deal
of eighteenth-century literature emphasizes, are those general pat-

terns—emotional, behavioral, psychological—that describe the commonality of mankind. This form of reasoning seeks similarity rather than difference, the predictable over the unusual, the explicit rather than the tacit, the general over the particular. If we just recall Hazlitt's working literary vocabulary—originality, genius, individual character, personal knowledge, nature, poetic imagination, power, force, expression, character, variety, passion—we can easily see why he must disagree with the view represented by Johnson. We are not just talking about a difference of opinion between Johnson and Hazlitt, but a fundamental shift in outlook. Contrasting his own view of Shakespeare—who is understandably the ultimate test case in English literature—with Johnson's didactic view, Hazlitt states that Johnson necessarily sees each character in Shakespeare's plays as "a species, instead of being an individual. He in fact found the general species or *didactic* form in Shakespeare's characters, which was all he sought or cared for; he did not find the individual traits, or *dramatic* distinctions which Shakespear has engrafted on this general nature, because he felt no interest in them" (4:176).

Hazlitt is not denying the general nature of literature's appeal. Much like Johnson, he recognizes in his essay "On Reason and Imagination" that "Man is (so to speak) an endless and infinitely varied repetition. . . . Our feeling of general humanity is at once an aggregate of a thousand different truths, and it is also the same truth a thousand times told" (12:55). But Hazlitt is also saying that such general views, in the abstract, are the business of philosophy, not literature. In other words, such general views are not what initially attracts us to literature. Reason may lead us, as it did Johnson, to an interest in the didactic elements of literature, but the imagination—whose primacy Hazlitt has been credited with "rediscovering"[8]—stimulates our interest in the dramatic elements. All those attributes of the dramatic imagination—"truth of nature," emphasis on the particular and local, character as individual expression, passion as spontaneity, and the basically tacit appeal of literature—have at their foundation the conviction that the power of feeling, whose intensity Hazlitt calls "gusto," is the heart of imaginative expression. Throughout his life and writings Hazlitt never wavered in his belief that "What does not touch the heart, or come home to the feelings, goes comparatively for little or nothing" (12:50). Judging by the response—past and present—to his own writings, it is clear that Hazlitt, however controversially, did indeed "touch the heart" and "come home to the feelings" of many readers.

Conclusion

As we reflect on Hazlitt's present reputation, we must keep steadily in mind his lifelong commitment to the dramatic imagination as both an artistic and moral vehicle. He must be judged in light of this commitment. Given the controversial and combative nature of his temperament, ideas, and writing style, it is no surprise to say that he may have alienated as many readers as he enlightened. Still, the key question is, how can we fairly assess Hazlitt's impact in his diverse roles as lecturer, journalist, critic, moralist, and essayist?

One obvious criterion is to look at how much his work has been discussed and by whom it has been examined. Measured against this standard, Hazlitt has done extremely well. The research of P. P. Howe has led to an excellent edition of Hazlitt's works, one that has made the range of his interests conveniently accessible. As a consequence, Hazlitt has been well served by James Houck's essential reference guide, which documents Hazlitt's rise as a major figure. In addition, there have been published, especially in the twentieth century, a number of excellent articles and books, many of which approach Hazlitt from a variety of angles. The major critical impetus behind the serious modern evaluation of Hazlitt began with P. P. Howe and Elisabeth Schneider and gained momentum with the invaluable work of W. P. Albrecht, Walter Jackson Bate, and John Bullitt. These authors, together with several others, clearly established Hazlitt as a major writer and critic who represented and assesssed the strengths and weaknesses of the romantic movement. In fact, any comprehensive examination of Wordsworth, Shelley, Byron, Coleridge, and Scott simply has to reckon with what Hazlitt said about these authors, In part, Hazlitt's independent assessment of the romantics has led to his reexamination by such distinguished critics as Herschel Baker, David Bromwich, John Kinnaird, and Roy Park. Not only have they discussed Hazlitt as a major figure in his own right, but also they have convincingly demonstrated that the romantic movement cannot be adequately understood without considering Hazlitt's role in that movement. Of the principal romantic critics, for example, Hazlitt remains the sole rival to Samuel Taylor Coleridge, a view that no doubt would have amused Hazlitt.

If we view Hazlitt's contributions as a prose stylist and essayist, we can safely argue that he holds a major place in the tradition of periodical essayists dating back to Montaigne. This tradition, which Hazlitt understood, mastered, and refined, developed in the eighteenth century with such writers as Richard Steele, Joseph Addison, Samuel Johnson, and Oliver Goldsmith. After Hazlitt, the tradition was maintained and advanced by such major figures as Matthew Arnold, T. S. Eliot, Lionel Trilling, and F. R. Leavis. This kind of writing often combined personal expression with literary, moral, and cultural criticism. Its principal purpose was to educate the public into an awareness of the essential contribution that literature of all kinds makes to the quality of life and to the central values of civilization. Like his predecessors and successors, Hazlitt was, above all, a humanist—a man whose focus, however polemic, was continually on human needs and values.

Seen as a man of letters, Hazlitt also ranks as a major figure. He is surely the equal of Samuel Johnson, Samuel Coleridge, or Matthew Arnold. Hazlitt wrote well and powerfully on aesthetics, moral theory, epistemology, drama, poetry, the novel, painting, economics, and political theory. Such a list does not include his original contributions as a periodical essayist. Hazlitt's writings combined breadth and depth. He began his career as a man who held to certain fundamental principles—literary, moral, aesthetic, political—and these principles allowed him to expand and deepen his views. However controversially, his works speak to the present time, a position gratifyingly reaffirmed by Kinnaird's and Bromwich's recent books.

When all is said and done, what strikes us most forcefully about Hazlitt the man and writer is his independence and integrity. As Michael Foot has recently commented, "The Hazlitt who so cherished his consistency was always listening for the new truth, and had an exceptional capacity for holding two opposing ideas in his mind at the same time."[9] Hazlitt could be repetitious, he could be contentious, he could be unfair; but he was always himself, speaking as the just man who was often in the minority. The fundamental integrity of his writings—the attribute that assures his continued importance—is that his independence and energetic vision encourage his readers to reassert their own individuality.

The highest compliment one can pay to Hazlitt is that as a man and a writer he was of a piece. Although he spoke and wrote in the various roles of lecturer, journalist, essayist, philosopher, and polemicist, his works are informed by a single voice—a voice as forceful and memorable as those of Samuel Johnson and Edmund Burke. This voice is what modern critics have come to acknowledge as one of Hazlitt's commanding strengths and one of his greatest contributions to English literature. Hazlitt is a unique writer, whose gifts for powerful expression, concise analysis, and controversial commitment guarantee his place as a major figure in the history of English letters. He wrote both wisely and well.

Notes and References

Preface

    1. W. P. Albrecht, *Hazlitt and the Creative Imagination* (Lawrence, Kans., 1965), 5–6.

Chapter One

    1. *The Complete Works of William Hazlitt,* 21 vols., ed. P. P. Howe (London and Toronto, 1930–34), 17:110. All further references are cited within the text.

    2. Ralph M. Wardle, *Hazlitt* (Lincoln, Nebr., 1971), 3.

    3. Russell E. Richey, "The Origins of British Radicalism: The Changing Rationale for Dissent," *Eighteenth Century Studies* 7 (1973–74):185.

    4. Ursula Henriques, *Religious Toleration in England 1787–1833* (Toronto: University of Toronto, 1961), 13.

    5. Quoted in *Religious Toleration in England,* 21.

    6. H. T. Dickinson, *Liberty and Property* (London: Weidenfeld and Nicolson, 1977), 15.

    7. Ibid., 61–62.

    8. Ibid., 202.

    9. Herschel Baker, *William Hazlitt* (Cambridge, Mass., 1962), 6.

    10. *The Letters of William Hazlitt,* ed. Herschel Moreland Sikes, William Hallam Bonner; and Gerald Lahey (London, 1979), 218–19. Hereafter cited as *Letters*.

Chapter Two

    1. William Godwin, *The Enquirer* (New York: Augustus M. Kelley, 1965), v–vi.

    2. *The Complete Works of Hannah More,* 2 vols. (New York: Harper, 1843), 1:61–62. See also Carl B. Cone, *The English Jacobins* (New York: Scribner's, 1968), 149–50.

    3. William Godwin, *Enquiry Concerning Political Justice,* ed. Isaac Kramnick (Baltimore: Penguin Books, 1976), 251–52. Hereafter cited as *PJ*. Kramnick's edition is based on Godwin's final revised edition of 1798.

    4. In *The Enquirer,* Godwin clarifies the relationship between sincerity and benevolence, arguing that "Sincerity is also a means, and is valuable so far as it answers the purposes of benevolence; benevolence is substantive" (341).

5. In *Hazlitt and The Spirit of the Age* (Oxford, 1971), Roy Park observes: "In Locke's conceptualism and in the nominalism of Hobbes, Berkeley, and Hume, abstraction is conceived as a process of generalization. In Hazlitt, on the other hand, abstraction is a process of individuation. . . . For Hazlitt, *all* our ideas are abstract. . . . Abstraction, accordingly, is a category of the human mind—a built-in principle of perceptual ordering" (97–98).

6. J. D. O'Hara, "Hazlitt and The Function of the Imagination," *PMLA* 81 (1966):556. O'Hara further notes that "The imagination's sympathetic ability enables us . . . to escape our solipsistic selves and enter disinterestedly into another person's concerns. Its existence in us is therefore a conclusive argument against those who believe man to be inherently and inescapably self-centered" (555).

7. Park, *Hazlitt and the Spirit of the Age,* 46–47.

8. In his excellent and provocative study, *William Hazlitt* (New York, 1978), John Kinnaird has extensively examined the role of a "primal power-urge" (89) in Hazlitt's works. There is no question that this is a central concept in Hazlitt's works and that it is linked with Hazlitt's idea of the imagination. However, Kinnaird frequently overstates his case, as when he argues that for Hazlitt "a contradiction in tendency naturally exists between poetic imagination . . . and the values of a humane morality" (110–11).

Chapter Three

1. John Kinnaird, "The Forgotten Self," *Partisan Review* 30 (1963):304.

2. Ibid., 304.

3. Albrecht, *Hazlitt and the Creative Imagination,* 31.

4. Ibid., 147. Earlier Albrecht comments on Hazlitt's "belief that the good poet, like the good citizen, must fulfill the possibilities of his imagination: that poetic structure, like the best government, requires an escape from egotism into imaginative completeness" (129).

5. Michael Polanyi, *The Tacit Dimension* (New York: Anchor Books, 1967), 4–5, 16–18. Like Hazlitt, Polanyi realizes the "difficulty [of finding] a stable alternative to [the] ideal of objectivity" (25).

6. Ibid., 62–63.

7. Park, *Hazlitt and the Spirit of the Age,* 164. See also *Hazlitt and the Creative Imagination,* where Albrecht remarks that "In modern times, Hazlitt thought the direction of speculative thought had diluted the affections and restricted the imagination" (53); and see Elisabeth Schneider, *The Aesthetics of William Hazlitt* (Philadelphia, 1933; reprinted in 1957), who argues that "it was one of the most consistent purposes of Hazlitt's life to compel the world to a recognition of feeling as a central fact in human existence" (36).

Chapter Four

1. Ian Jack, *English Literature 1815–1832* (Oxford 1963), 268.
2. Ibid., 268.
3. For other views of Hazlitt's concept of "the spirit of the age," see Patrick Story, "Hazlitt's Definition of the Spirit of the Age," *Wordsworth Circle* 6 (1975), who argues that Hazlitt "defines the spirit of the age . . . as a dualistic struggle between the historical progress of intellect . . . and the natural 'infirmities' of an implied static 'human nature'" (99); Albrecht, *Hazlitt and the Creative Imagination,* who suggests that the spirit of the age "is not just one thing: it is change in general, and reform in particular; it is the rage for novelty but paradoxically it is also a return to prejudice; it is self-love and disinterestedness; it is the clash between change and reaction which was unresolved in individuals as well as in public affairs" (62); and Park, *Hazlitt and the Spirit of the Age,* who asserts that "The opposition between poetry and science in the early nineteenth century is the most significant single characteristic of the period" (2).
4. Baker, *William Hazlitt,* 61–62.

Chapter Five

1. Thomas DeQuincey, "Alexander Pope," in *DeQuincey as Critic,* ed. John E. Jordan (London: Routledge and Kegan Paul, 1973), 269.
2. DeQuincey, "Alexander Pope," 269.
3. W. Jackson Bate, *The Burden of the Past and the English Poet* (New York: Norton, 1972), 48. Over the years, Bate has been one of the strongest advocates of Hazlitt's value as a literary critic. See Bate's introductory essay on Hazlitt in *Criticism: The Major Texts* (New York, 1952), 281–92.
4. Bate, *The Burden of the Past and the English Poet,* 4.
5. Ibid., 3.
6. I am here referring to two books by Harold Bloom: *The Anxiety of Influence* (New York: Oxford, 1973) and *A Map of Misreading* (New York: Oxford, 1975). In the former book Bloom argues that "*Poetic influence—when it involves two strong, authentic poets—always proceeds by a misreading of the prior poet, an act of creative correction that is actually and necessarily a misinterpretation*" (30). In the latter book, Bloom hints at how his idea of poetic influence can be applied just as forcefully to critical influence, a matter I take up when I deal with Samuel Johnson's influence on Hazlitt. Bloom writes that influence "means that there are *no* texts, but only relationships *between* texts. These relationships depend upon a critical act, a misreading or misprision . . . that does not differ in kind from the necessary critical acts performed by every strong reader upon every text he encounters" (3).

7. See John Kinnaird, "Hazlitt, Keats, and the Poetics of Intersubjectivity," *Criticism* 19 (1977):1–16 for a discussion of the idea of poetry "as something distinct from, and existing antecedently to, poetic texts and their creation" (1). Kinnaird's essay is substantially reprinted in his book *William Hazlitt*.

8. Charles I. Patterson, Jr., "William Hazlitt as a Critic of Prose Fiction," *PMLA* 68 (1953):1001, 1003.

9. Park, *Hazlitt and the Spirit of the Age,* 38. For a differing view of Hazlitt as a critic who failed to appreciate the importance of "organic unity," see Charles I. Patterson, Jr., "Hazlitt's Criticism in Retrospect," *Studies in English Literature* 21 (1981):647–63.

10. Bloom, *The Anxiety of Influence,* 11.

11. On Hazlitt's affective understanding of Shakespeare's drama, see the following essays: W. P. Albrecht, "Hazlitt, Passion, and *King Lear,*" *Studies in English Literature* 18 (1978):611–24; and John Kinnaird, "Hazlitt and the 'Design' of Shakespearean Tragedy: A 'Character' Critic Revisited," in *Shakespeare Quarterly,* 28 (1977):22–39.

12. Samuel Johnson, "Preface to Shakespeare," in *Johnson on Shakespeare,* ed. Arthur Sherbo, The Yale Edition of the Writings of Samuel Johnson (New Haven: Yale, 1968), 7:71.

Chapter Six

1. Baker, *William Hazlitt,* 392.

2. See David Bromwich, "The Originality of Hazlitt's Essays," *Yale Review* 72 (1983):366–84. See also Bromwich's *Hazlitt: The Mind of a Critic* (New York, 1984).

3. For a revealing discussion of how Montaigne developed a self through his personal essays, see Frederick Rider, *The Dialectic of Selfhood in Montaigne* (Stanford: Stanford University Press, 1973).

4. Jack, *English Literature 1815–1832,* 273–74.

5. Albrecht, *Hazlitt and the Creative Imagination,* 161–62, 164.

6. For a thorough examination of *Table-Talk,* see Robert Ready, *Hazlitt at Table* (Rutherford, 1981).

7. In praising Cobbett, Hazlitt was also commending a writer who shared his own antagonism for Thomas Malthus. See John W. Osborne, *William Cobbett* (New Brunswick: Rutgers, 1966), 114–19.

8. In *The Aesthetics of William Hazlitt,* Elisabeth Schneider has commented that "Hazlitt was himself first of all a product of eighteenth–century 'common sense'" (85). To a limited extent, this observation is true, so long as we focus on Hazlitt's personal essays.

9. Kinnaird, *William Hazlitt,* 272.

10. Baker, *William Hazlitt,* 200. Baker continues: "On everything he

has his own opinion, and he expounds it with the blunt authority that became the touchstone of his style" (201).

11. R. P. Bond, *The Tatler* (Cambridge, Mass.: Harvard University, 1971), 142–43. For a comprehensive survey of the traditional uses of character writing, see the two books by Benjamin Boyce: *The Theophrastan Character in England to 1642* (Cambridge, Mass.: Harvard University, 1947) and *The Polemic Character 1640–1661* (Lincoln: University of Nebraska, 1955).

12. Jack, *English Literature 1815–1832,* 269.

13. Patrick Story's approach, in "Emblems of Infirmity: Contemporary Portraits in Hazlitt's *The Spirit of the Age,*" *Wordsworth Circle* 10 (1979):81–90, may be extended to many of Hazlitt's familiar essays.

14. Hazlitt was not alone among his contemporaries in his praise of Napoleon. At one time or another, Byron, Godwin, Leigh Hunt, and Elizabeth Inchbald—to name some of Hazlitt's contemporaries—share Hazlitt's estimate of Napoleon. For details, see E. Tangye Lean, *The Napoleonists* (London: Oxford, 1970).

Chapter Seven

1. Kinnaird, *William Hazlitt,* 368–69. Kinnaird further contends that "Hazlitt enters criticism at a time when a new relationship with the reader was called for, when the last illusion of a privileged public authority in criticism—the throne of Right Reason occupied by Dr. Johnson—had crumbled away" (169–70).

2. Johnson, "Preface to Shakespeare," 7:71.

3. Jack, *English Literature 1815–1832,* 270, 273.

4. John L. Mahoney, *The Logic of Passion,* rev. ed. (New York, 1981), 28.

5. Albrecht, *Hazlitt and the Creative Imagination,* 66.

6. Park, *Hazlitt and the Spirit of the Age,* 192.

7. Ibid., 38.

8. Kinnaird, *William Hazlitt,* 61.

9. Michael Foot, "Critic and Crusader," *The New Republic* (12 March 1984):34.

Selected Bibliography

PRIMARY SOURCES

Howe, P. P., ed. *The Complete Works of William Hazlitt.* 21 vols. London and
    Toronto: J. M. Dent and Sons, 1930–34.
Sikes, Herschel Moreland; William Hallam Bonner; and Gerald Lahey, eds.
    The Letters of William Hazlitt. London: Macmillan, 1979.

SECONDARY SOURCES

1. Bibliography
Houck, James A., ed. *William Hazlitt: A Reference Guide.* Boston: G. K.
    Hall & Co., 1977. An indispensable annotated bibliography that covers
    the period 1805–1973.

2. Books and Articles
Albrecht, W. P. *Hazlitt and the Creative Imagination.* Lawrence: University
    of Kansas, 1965. A major discussion of Hazlitt's concept of the
    imagination.
————. "Hazlitt, Passion, and *King Lear.*" *Studies in English Literature* 18
    (1978):611–624. Discusses Hazlitt's affective understanding of tragedy.
Baker, Herschel. *William Hazlitt.* Cambridge, Mass.: Harvard University,
    1962. One of the best books on Hazlitt; particularly strong on Hazlitt's
    thought.
Bate, Walter Jackson. "William Hazlitt." In *Criticism: The Major Texts,*
    281–92. New York: Harcourt, Brace & World, 1952. An essential ex-
    amination of the key concepts in Hazlitt's literary criticism.
Bromwich, David. *Hazlitt: The Mind of a Critic.* New York: Oxford Uni-
    versity Press, 1984. The most impressive and comprehensive modern
    study of Hazlitt—at once informative, thoughtful, and engaging.
————. "The Originality of Hazlitt's Essays." *Yale Review* 72 (1983):366–
    84. An important study of Hazlitt's use of the familiar essay as a way of
    exploring "how his self-knowledge is a condition of his knowledge of the
    world."

Bryson, Norman. "Hazlitt on Painting." *Journal of Aesthetics and Art Criticism* 37 (1978):37–45. Discusses Hazlitt's understanding of the visual arts in relation to Augustan and romantic aesthetics.

Bullitt, John M. "Hazlitt and the Romantic Conception of the Imagination." *Philological Quarterly* 24 (1945):343–61. Discusses Hazlitt's emphasis on the sympathetic power of the imagination.

Howe, P. P. *The Life of William Hazlitt.* New York: George H. Doran, 1922. An informative guide to Hazlitt's life.

Jack, Ian. *English Literature 1815–1832.* Oxford: Clarendon Press, 1963. A strong defense of Hazlitt as a major critic.

Kinnaird, John. "The Forgotten Self." *Partisan Review* 30 (1963):302–6. An aggressive assertion of Hazlitt's importance as a writer.

———. "Hazlitt and the 'Design' of Shakespearean Tragedy: A 'Character' Critic Revisited." *Shakespeare Quarterly* 28 (1977):22–39. Examines Hazlitt's understanding of the dramatic imagination.

———. "Hazlitt, Keats, and the Poetics of Intersubjectivity." *Criticism* 19 (1977):1–16. A controversial study of Hazlitt's idea of poetry as "something distinct from, and existing antecedently to, poetic texts and their creation."

———. *William Hazlitt.* New York: Columbia, 1978. A provocative and comprehensive discussion of the role of power in Hazlitt's thought.

Mahoney, John L. *The Logic of Passion.* New York: Fordham University, 1981. A lucid introduction to certain key terms in Hazlitt's criticism.

O'Hara, J.D. "Hazlitt and The Functions of the Imagination." *PMLA* 81 (1966):552–62. Deals with the diverse roles of the sympathetic imagination in Hazlitt's works.

Park, Roy. *Hazlitt and the Spirit of the Age.* Oxford: Clarendon Press, 1971. An important study of Hazlitt's lifelong opposition to abstract thought.

Patterson, Charles I., Jr. "Hazlitt's Criticism in Retrospect." *Studies in English Literature* 21 (1981):647–63. A revaluation of Hazlitt's criticism, arguing that Hazlitt failed to understand the importance of "organic unity."

———. "William Hazlitt as a Critic of Prose Fiction." *PMLA* 68 (1953):1001–16. Argues persuasively that Hazlitt is one of the first important critics of the novel.

Ready, Robert. *Hazlitt at Table.* Rutherford: Fairleigh Dickinson University, 1981. A comprehensive study of *Table-Talk* in which Hazlitt's presence as an essayist is "the central unifying and problematic concern of the book."

Schneider, Elisabeth. *The Aesthetics of William Hazlitt.* 1933. Reprint. Philadelphia: University of Pennsylvania, 1957. An early study, dealing with Hazlitt's theory in relation to late eighteenth- and early nineteenth-century aesthetic thought.

Story, Patrick. "Emblems of Infirmity: Contemporary Portraits in Hazlitt's *The Spirit of the Age.*" *Wordsworth Circle* 10 (1979):81–90. A revealing essay on Hazlitt as a moral character-writer.

Wardle, Ralph M. *Hazlitt.* Lincoln: University of Nebraska, 1971. A useful survey of Hazlitt's life and writings.

Wordsworth Circle 6 (1975). A special issue on William Hazlitt.

Index